K-ZOO NEWS

On-the-Spot Reports From the Wild Side

Ron Coffen

Pacific Press Publishing Association
Boise, Idaho
Oshawa, Ontario, Canada

Edited by Jerry D. Thomas
Designed by Dennis Ferree
Cover and inside illustrations by Kim Justinen
Typeset in 10/12 Century Schoolbook

Library of Congress Cataloging-in-Publication Data:
Coffen, Ron, 1969-
K-ZOO news: on the spot reports from the wild side / Ron Coffen.
p. cm.
Summary: A reporter for the "Zoo News" interviews a variety of animals, asking them about their homes, habits, and habitats.
ISBN 0-8163-1086-6
1. Animals—Miscellanea—Juvenile literature. [1. Animals. 2. Questions and answers.] I. Title.
QL49.C6714 1992
591—dc20 91-38242
CIP
AC

92 93 94 95 96 • 5 4 3 2 1

Table of Contents

Giraffology 7
No Dumb Bird 11
Peek-A-Booby 17
Tusk, Tusk, Tusk 22
Prairie Pooch 27
Crazy Critter 31
Life Otter Be Fun! 35
Mr. P of the Cat World 39
Tern Style 45
Desert Ship 49
Crazy Mixed-up Bird 53
Rabbitroos? Kangabits? 57
His Bill Holds More . . . 61
Haymakers 66
Just the Facts 70
Boomers and Fliers 75
Dizzy Des, the Littler Riddler 81
Is This Fox Fur Real? 85

The Bird That Can't Fly 89
No Big Deal 94
Lighten Up! 98
Nature's Teddy Bear 103
A Star Performance 107
Monster Guinea Pigs 111
Doxiongmao 115
Prickly Football 121
Solar Snowball 125

Dedication

I dedicate this book to:
My mother, who convinced me this was good writing!
My father, who counseled me at so many points!
Kathryn, who has supported me with her
encouragement, prayers, and laughter!
My King, who has given me the subject matter
for this book!

Giraffology

K-ZOO NEWS: Hi, there! This is your friendly news reporter coming to you with another fascinating story! I am located today in the middle of a large herd of trees—oh! . . . sorry . . . giraffes. Uh, sir? (No answer.) Excuse me, sir. (No answer.) *Hey, you up there*!

JEROME: Huh? What was that? I think we're having an earthquake; I felt the ground rumble. Oh, no, that's not it. Someone's down there, I think. Wonder what he wants.

K-ZOO NEWS: Excuse me, sir, but could I interview you?

JEROME: Hmmm . . . winterlew? I don't know what a winterlew is.

K-ZOO NEWS: *Interview*!

JEROME: Oh! Yes, by all means.

K-ZOO NEWS: Thank you. Could you take off your stilts before we start?

JEROME: Not to be rude, sir, but no. I don't really think that's at all possible, sir. These legs are a rather permanent part of my body. You didn't think I was built with Legos, did you?

K-ZOO NEWS: No, I guess not. But your legs must be six feet long! And your neck is even longer!

JEROME: I think you must be the most perceptive interviewer I've ever met! Actually, you're the only interviewer I've ever met.

K-ZOO NEWS: Well, sir, I'd estimate you were fourteen feet tall!

JEROME: Hey, come on now! It's not polite to make fun of the faults of others. Now, I do believe you owe me an apology for such inconsiderate behavior! Just because I'm a runt doesn't mean you can poke fun at me.

K-ZOO NEWS: Runt? I certainly didn't call you a runt! On the contrary! You are of magnificent height!

JEROME: I am? Not to contradict, but I'm not really, sir. I'm very short! You see, a lion attacked my mother when she was pregnant with me, and as a result, I was born extremely short. Ah! But my father. I want to be just like him! He is nineteen feet tall—just about as tall as we come!

K-ZOO NEWS: Ni—nine—nineteen feet tall? Whewwww! That's incredible!

JEROME: Yes, sir. We are the tallest land mammals in the entire world! Actually, the tallest land mammals in the entire universe, as far as we know.

K-ZOO NEWS: Well, I can't argue with that! Why the long neck, anyway?

JEROME: The reason that we have a long neck is a secret! But we make very good use of this advantage. We peer over the tops of trees to keep track of each other. We also eat the leaves and branches of the acacia trees. With our long necks we can easily reach the leaves. And, as if our long neck wasn't enough, we've been equipped with a seventeen-inch tongue! That's probably longer than the distance from your middle finger to your elbow!

K-ZOO NEWS: You eat from the acacia tree? That can't be! Acacia trees have razor-sharp thorns!

JEROME: They do? Hmmm. I guess you're right, come to think of it, but I'd never noticed before.

K-ZOO NEWS: You haven't? Well, look at you! You have thousands of those thorns sticking in your skin!

JEROME: Well, look at that! You're right! Wonder how long I've had those. No wonder people don't usually eat us!

K-ZOO NEWS: I've read in many places that you are the "voiceless" animal.

JEROME: Oh, dear me, no! Not at all. Our call is somewhere between the bleat of a sheep and the moo of a cow. I suppose people think we have no voices because we rarely use them. We have excellent control of our tongues, which is more than I can say of most humans!

K-ZOO NEWS: Sadly true. Say, tell me about your family.

JEROME: We have one calf. He's a beauty! When he was born, he was just six feet tall and only weighed 150 pounds. When he grows up, he may weigh as much as 4,000 pounds. That's probably how much your family car weighs!

K-ZOO NEWS: Just six feet?! Only 150 pounds!? Are you serious? Four thousand pounds? How do you get to weigh so much?

JEROME: What most people don't know is that giraffes drink little if any water. The area of Africa in which we live is without water part of the year. But we do eat as much as seventy-five pounds of food a day. Actually, we eat that seventy-five pounds of food several times a day. You see, the food is so good the first time, we bring it back up and try it again (like cows do when they chew their cud).

K-ZOO NEWS: Seventy-five pounds? That's about what forty-two trash bags full of leaves weigh! When do you find time to sleep when you eat like that?

JEROME: Don't worry! We can go twenty-four hours without a wink of sleep! When we do close our eyes, we only really sleep for an hour or so, and we sleep standing up.

K-ZOO NEWS: You're kidding! What an animal!

JEROME: Now let me tell you some things you didn't know about giraffes (although I don't think you knew too much to begin with. This'll probably all be new for you).

- Our blood pressure is two to three times that of humans. Because we have ten- to twelve-foot necks, our hearts have to force blood through our necks to our brains against gravity. Because of this, our hearts are huge. They weigh twenty-five pounds, are two feet long, and have walls three inches thick.
- Giraffes have horns! We have two to five skin-covered, stubby horns on our heads.
- Despite the length of our necks, we have the same number of vertebrae as a guinea pig! Only ours are a good deal larger, of course.
- We can gallop at speeds up to thirty miles per hour!
- Because of their keen sense of hearing, the females keep watch for enemies.
- Julius Caesar is reported to have exhibited a giraffe in Rome, and we also appear in ancient Egyptian manuscripts!

K-ZOO NEWS: What fascinating facts, Mr. Giraffe! Thank you for your time. That's our report from giraffe country. Stay tuned for more K-ZOO News after these messages.

No Dumb Bird

K-ZOO NEWS: I'm standing here in the grasslands of Africa with the world's largest living bird! Isn't that right, sir?

ORVILLE: Well, I do believe that's correct. Ostriches are considered the largest.

K-ZOO NEWS: I once interviewed what I thought was a flightless bird—that was the Adélie penguin—and he corrected me by insisting that he was quite capable of flying—underwater. Now, with all due respect to you, sir, I was informed that you are truly a flightless bird. Is that so?

ORVILLE: I suppose that's correct. Because of our weight, it's quite impossible for our small wings to get us off the ground.

K-ZOO NEWS: Do you have any enemies?

ORVILLE: Enemies? I should say so! It seems someone or something is always after us! If it's not a lion or a cheetah after us at high speed, it's the humans!

K-ZOO NEWS: Humans? Boy! You must really do a lot of interviews!

ORVILLE: Well, I'm afraid, my friend, that the humans chasing us aren't usually interviewers like yourself. They come rampaging after us with rifles and horses until we're exhausted.

K-ZOO NEWS: Who are these humans, and why do they chase you?!

ORVILLE: Our human enemies are Arabian sheiks who get bored with oil wells and decide to go after ostrich feathers. Even English tourists used to hunt us just for the sport! Before the sheiks and tourists, we were sought because our feathers represented royalty. The fair ladies of ancient Rome valued our feathers as highly as they did their slaves! Knights would decorate their helmets with our feathers, and in later times, women decorated their hats with feathers. Ostrich feathers sold for as much as five hundred dollars a pound in the 1800s. The price has gone down considerably now (not as many knights or royalty, you know), but people still seem to like ostrich plumes.

K-ZOO NEWS: With enemies like that, who needs friends, right?

ORVILLE: Huh?

K-ZOO NEWS: Never mind. Anyway, if I had so many enemies and was practically wingless, I guess I'd stick my head in the sand too!

ORVILLE: Stick your head in the sand? Would you look silly! Why would you do a crazy thing like that?

K-ZOO NEWS: Well, I thought that's what you did when you were scared.

ORVILLE: Ha! No, no, no.

K-ZOO NEWS: But—but I thought—

ORVILLE: Why, sonny, you must have the brains of a turkey (domesticated, that is)! Oh, I know you've heard all sorts of rumors. Those sheiks will do anything for a laugh, and now they've filled your mind with nonsense! There are several false stories. One tells of an ostrich who believed himself to be concealed when he put his head behind a stone because then, he couldn't see his enemy. A similar story tells of an ostrich who figured that if he couldn't see his enemy, then his enemy couldn't see him. So this ostrich stuck his head in the sand! Have you ever heard such farfetched stories in your life? We might be one of the dumber birds, but we aren't stupid! What does a bird have to do to get any respect around here?

K-ZOO NEWS: Well—er—I was told that you are an exceedingly stupid bird. So what's the real story? How *do* you get away from your enemies? I mean, pardon me for beating a dead horse, but I needn't tell you that you can't fly.

ORVILLE: Well, you can't fly either! What would you do? Huh?

K-ZOO NEWS: Well . . .

ORVILLE: Run! We run! I admit, ostriches are easily frightened and are sometimes known to run around like they were crazy. But when an ostrich takes off at twenty-seven miles per hour, no human can catch us on foot, no matter if we're strategically planning an escape route or just running around in circles! And let me tell you, twenty-seven miles per hour is a mere trot for us! When those barbaric sheiks come after us with rifles and horses, we don't run for a hole in the sand! We make tracks out of there at speeds of up to forty miles per hour. And we don't take just little steps. At full speed, our stride stretches out to almost twenty-eight feet! Those money-hungry sheiks expect to lose two or more horses in the process of catching just one ostrich! You see, the sheiks chase us until we're exhausted, then grab us. We kick with our legs and put up quite a fight. It's not pretty.

K-ZOO NEWS: Sounds like quite a life! Do you have a family?

ORVILLE: Yes. I have thirty children and—

K-ZOO NEWS: What? Thirty kids?

ORVILLE: That's right. Would you like to see their pictures?

K-ZOO NEWS: Uh, maybe later. How did you end up with thirty?

ORVILLE: Well, as I was about to explain, several females contribute to my nest. As a matter of fact, they fight over who gets to sit on the eggs. After the eggs hatch, I take care of the kids.

K-ZOO NEWS: That's a lot of mouths to feed!

ORVILLE: Oh, it's not so bad. There's plenty of grass, herbs, insects, and small reptiles to fill our stomachs.

K-ZOO NEWS: You are thought to be a rather silent bird. Would you care to voice your opinion on that?

ORVILLE: Silent? Well, we don't use our voices very often, but when we do, it's certainly far from silent. David Livingstone commented that our bellowings were frequently difficult to distinguish from the roaring of a lion!

K-ZOO NEWS: I must say, you seem to be a very fascinating animal!

ORVILLE: Why, thank you! Let me tell you some things that you probably don't know about ostriches.

- A male ostrich may grow to a height of eight feet.
- We have superb vision and very long necks and can see our enemies coming while they are still at a distance.
- Because of this, zebras often mingle with an ostrich herd. When the herd is frightened and runs off, the zebras follow.
- An ostrich may weigh as much as 345 pounds! (Can you imagine 300 pounds moving across the desert at forty miles per hour?
- We lay the largest eggs in the world. One egg may weigh three-and-a-half pounds.

K-ZOO NEWS: I hate to stick your foot in your mouth, but in relation to your size, you lay the smallest egg. It weighs only 1 percent of the female's body weight.

ORVILLE: Shhh! Would you keep quiet?

K-ZOO NEWS: Forgive me for interrupting. Do go on.

ORVILLE: Well, ostriches have been trained by people for riding and pulling carts. But we tire easily, and then we simply sit down and quit. Besides that:

- We may live to be sixty years old. That's if the sheiks don't get us first!
- Because of our ability to reproduce, ten living ostriches may be hatched for each one destroyed by a rifle.
- Ostrich eggs have been found a foot under the sand!
- Ostriches are mentioned in Job 39:13-18. (Even the Bible writers considered us babbling idiots! Look it up and see!)

K-ZOO NEWS: Well, I never! So long, my hunted friend! This is your K-Zoo News reporter signing off after an exciting interview with an animal whose popularity comes from its goofy appearance.

ORVILLE: What?

K-ZOO NEWS: Well, it's true! Ask anyone!

ORVILLE: Now see here!

K-ZOO NEWS: Like I said, this is—

ORVILLE: I can't believe—

K-ZOO NEWS: —uh—signing off—

ORVILLE: How could you? After all we've been through together!

K-ZOO NEWS: —until next time . . .

Peek-A-Booby

K-ZOO NEWS: My job is on the rocks now. At any moment I expect to fall to my death from this extremely high and precarious perch among these rocky pinnacles. I must be a booby for accepting these bird assignments!

BREWSTER: Well, you don't look like a booby, and I should hope I don't look like you!

K-ZOO NEWS: Huh? What? Who are you? Wait! Don't come any closer. You're going to push me over the edge, aren't you?

BREWSTER: I'm a blue-footed booby, and I have no intention of pushing you over the edge. But now that you've mentioned it, that could be very entertaining.

K-ZOO NEWS: I have a sinking feeling that you're the booby bird I'm supposed to interview.

BREWSTER: Yes, I suppose I am.

K-ZOO NEWS: Well, let's start with the color of your feet. Why are they such a brilliant shade of blue?

BREWSTER: I don't know.

K-ZOO NEWS: You don't know? What do you mean, you don't know?

BREWSTER: I mean, I am unsure and uncertain as to the exact and specific purpose and reason for the color and hue of my feet.

K-ZOO NEWS: I don't think we've started off on the right foot. Look, quit playing games with me and tell me why your feet are blue!

BREWSTER: I don't *know.* Do you know why some people have pink, spiked hair?

K-ZOO NEWS: No.

BREWSTER: OK. There you go. I don't know why we have blue feet except that we've always had blue feet, we always will have blue feet, and I don't intend to give up blue feet on your account.

K-ZOO NEWS: Oh. Well, how about the booby part of your name? How'd you get a name like booby?

BREWSTER: Well, it's like this. Because we're not afraid of people, we've been known to rest on the rigging of ships and simply sit quietly until a hungry sailor grabs us. Man is our worst enemy, so when we don't run from him, people think we're as stupid as we look.

K-ZOO NEWS: Sounds pretty stupid to me.

BREWSTER: We aren't stupid. I prefer to think of it as bravery. Haven't you heard the saying *brave as a booby?*

K-ZOO NEWS: No, I haven't. And you're stupid.

BREWSTER: Brave!

K-ZOO NEWS: Stupid!

BREWSTER: Brave!

K-ZOO NEWS: Suicidal.

BREWSTER: Bad habits are hard to break.

K-ZOO NEWS: But your habit is going to kill you!

BREWSTER: Humans aren't any smarter. How many people die from the habit of smoking cigarettes?

K-ZOO NEWS: Hmmm. OK, OK. So, tell me where you live.

BREWSTER: Here?

K-ZOO NEWS: Well, we could walk over there, and you could tell me there, instead of here. My, you're difficult!

BREWSTER: I meant, I live here.

K-ZOO NEWS: Where?

BREWSTER: I live here—on the rocks.

K-ZOO NEWS: Could you be a little bit more specific?

BREWSTER: I live on the rocky shores of the Pacific coastlines of tropical America from Baja California to northern Peru. How was that for being specific?

K-ZOO NEWS: Good! Good! Now we're talkin'. Why do you live by the ocean?

BREWSTER: I like the scenery.

K-ZOO NEWS: Really?

BREWSTER: No, of course not! I live by the ocean because fish are harder to come by in the desert. And since I live by eating fish, the desert didn't seem too inviting.

K-ZOO NEWS: I see. What kind of fish do you like?

BREWSTER: Flying fish. Mmmmm, mmm, they're great!

K-ZOO NEWS: How do you catch your meals?

BREWSTER: With a fishing pole.

K-ZOO NEWS: You're kidding!

BREWSTER: Yes, I am.

K-ZOO NEWS: Oh. So how *do* you catch your meals?

BREWSTER: The way we catch flying fish is to follow a ship. Ships stir up the fish and cause them to jump out of the water. Then we plunge on a long slant and hit the water just as the flying fish duck back in.

K-ZOO NEWS: Wow! You're quite a booby trap for flying fish, aren't you?

BREWSTER: Oh, yes. Boobies are experts on the ocean. We cruise on the waves, keeping a sharp lookout for food. We're Olympic-quality divers. To catch fish other than flying fish, we fly fifty to one hundred feet above the water, where we keep an attentive eye turned below. We look especially for schools of fish. Suddenly, we head straight down and plunge headfirst into the water at one hundred feet per second. That's about seventy miles per hour! So if we started our dive from fifty feet, it would take us only half a second to reach the water—zero to sixty in five-tenths of a second! That's real acceleration! Eat my dust, Lamborghini!

We close our wings the moment before we strike the water, and then all that's left for the landlubbers to see is a little geyser where we hit the waves. We dive past the fish, as far as eighty feet below the water's surface, and then grab a meal in our bills while we're coming back to the surface. Our Spanish name is *piquero,* which means "that heads into the water." The Spanish weren't as rude as the sailors when they were handing out names for birds.

K-ZOO NEWS: How do you achieve that kind of speed so quickly?

BREWSTER: Gravity helps a lot. But our size is also significant. We are about thirty-five inches in length, with a long neck and sleek body that are perfect for diving. Our wingspan can reach more than five feet!

K-ZOO NEWS: Well, you're a strange bird!

BREWSTER: Yes, in several ways. Unlike other boobies that usually have white feathers, blue-footers like me keep an immature plumage appearance of white feathers below, brown with white spots above, and a large white patch on our upper back. We also have no nose openings or nostrils.

K-ZOO NEWS: So how do you breathe?

BREWSTER: We don't. We hold our breaths all our lives! That's why we're so short-lived.

K-ZOO NEWS: Is that right?

BREWSTER: No, it's not right! We breathe through a specially constructed palate instead of through nose openings like other birds do.

K-ZOO NEWS: Well, thanks for the interview. I'll let you take a breather.

BREWSTER: Sure.

K-ZOO NEWS: Until next time—

BREWSTER: Say, you wanna go cruise the waves with me?

K-ZOO NEWS: Uh, nah. I left my swimming trunks at home.

BREWSTER: Oh. Too bad.

K-ZOO NEWS: Yeah. I'm pretty broken up too. I feel just awful . . .

Tusk, Tusk, Tusk

K-ZOO NEWS: Tusks. That's what the boss said. Something about tusks. Good! I've always wanted to interview an elephant! But I'm terribly lost unless I'm to interview a woolly mammoth—I'm way up north. I could be in Alaska, Greenland, or eastern Canada! I'm freezing, and I think I'm going to sneeze . . . *Sniff, sniff!*

WALLY: Whatchya blubbering about there, son?

K-ZOO NEWS: I'm supposed to be interviewing elephants, and there aren't any elephants up here. The boss said tusks and—

WALLY: Tusks? Tusks? Did you say tusks?

K-ZOO NEWS: Yes, tusks. And then I find myself up here and—

WALLY: Well, I think I can help you out with the tusks. Look here, son. I've got tusks, yes sirree! I've got two of 'em—one on each side, see? How about that for a fine pair of chompers?

K-ZOO NEWS: Hey! Tusks enough! Yes, that's it! You're a walrus, aren't you?

WALLY: You're quick!

K-ZOO NEWS: Thanks. Hey, you wouldn't mind if I asked you a few questions, would you? Good! Now, let's see. Since we're on the subject, how'd you get those tusks, anyway?

WALLY: Well, I didn't steal 'em, if that's what you're thinking.

K-ZOO NEWS: Oh, no, sir, nothing like that!

WALLY: I grew 'em, of course. These here tusks, which can grow to be over three feet long, are actually very long teeth.

K-ZOO NEWS: Teeth? Wow! You should see an orthodontist. What do you do with those—those—teeth? I'm just curious, of course!

WALLY: Not to fear, my friend. These tusks are used as weapons, but not against humans. We use them to fight with other walruses during mating season. You know, we have to prove our strength. Those fights can get pretty heated too. Sometimes a walrus will lose a tusk in a battle. Walruses are peaceful animals at heart, and most of the time we just use our tusks to poke other walruses and tell them to get out of the way, or we use tusks to ward off attacks from polar bears. The tusks come in handy for getting out of the water too. We just hook our ivory teeth onto the edge of an ice floe and haul ourselves up. They're also useful for digging up delicious shellfish from the bottom of the ocean.

K-ZOO NEWS: Wait a second! Hold on! You eat shellfish? Aren't those tiny little creatures?

WALLY: Yup. We eat little animals such as crabs, clams, and shrimp. We eat worms, too, but our favorite food is the clam. Ummm, ummm! Boy, I'd like to sink my tusks into a clam right now.

K-ZOO NEWS: You must have to eat a lot of clams to keep your weight up.

WALLY: True, very true! You see, walruses weigh from 1,500 to 4,800 pounds and are ten to fifteen feet long. Our skin—or blubber, that is—is about six inches thick. Blubber makes up about a third of our weight. So if I weighed

4,000 pounds, 1,300 pounds would be pure blubber! To keep ourselves pleasantly plump, we have to eat about 100 pounds of food a day. It turns out that as many as 10,000 clams a day die for a noble cause—breakfast, lunch, and supper for one walrus.

K-ZOO NEWS: Where do you find all these clams?

WALLY: Oh, about 300 feet under water. There, at the bottom of the ocean, we use our tongues to form a sort of vacuum that sucks clams into our mouths.

K-ZOO NEWS: You walruses must be good swimmers to get 300 feet under water.

WALLY: We aren't bad, really. We can swim at a speed of five miles an hour. Our feet are actually flippers, and that makes us good swimmers. When we have to move, we often will just climb onto an ice floe and let it float us to where we want to go. In the winter and spring we spend much of our time dozing and soaking up some rays on the beaches with many thousands of neighboring walruses.

K-ZOO NEWS: Sounds pretty lazy to me.

WALLY: Lazy? Oh, I don't know about that. If you weighed two tons (4,000 pounds!), you wouldn't want to run around willy-nilly here and there all day either.

K-ZOO NEWS: You have a point. Hey, what's that bobbing in the water over there?

WALLY: Oh, that's a walrus taking a nap. We sometimes sleep in the water standing up. We have two air pouches under our throats that we can fill with air until they're the size of beach balls. Then we close our eyes and just float away into dreamland.

K-ZOO NEWS: Fascinating, fascinating. Say, I've heard that the walrus population is dwindling to a dangerously low level.

WALLY: I'm afraid so, son. We are often ruthlessly hunted down for our ivory tusks and our blubber. Much of the time the hunters sell our blubber to companies that make dog food out of it. How about that, huh? We don't multiply like rabbits, either. We generally have only one pup every two years. So, I'm afraid our numbers are indeed dwindling.

K-ZOO NEWS: What a shame. So all of you out there, if you see a walrus, keep your dog away from him, OK? Well, thank you for this interview, Wally. Until the next K-ZOO News, aloha.

WALLY: Aloha? That's for Hawaii.

K-ZOO NEWS: Oh, well, then, adios.

WALLY: Adios? That's Spanish.

K-ZOO NEWS: Look! I don't care! Just let these guys get on to the next story, OK?

WALLY: Oh, all right. Go away, already!

Prairie Pooch

K-ZOO NEWS: Hello, pardner! I'm your friendly news reporter coming at you from some strange surroundings. I'm standing in the middle of what appears to be hundreds of tiny volcanoes where . . .

SLIM: Hey, buddy! Let's move it out! Come on! Scram! Nothing to see here! Beat it, buster! Adios, aloha, au revoir, and out ya go!

K-ZOO NEWS: Excuse me, sir. I wonder if I could interview you?

SLIM: Interview! Me? Yes, yes, sure! Interview! Oh, yes! Let's do have an interview. I so much like interviews! At least I think I do. When can we start? Can we start now? Huh? Huh? Can we? Could we? Would we? I'm so excited! Hey, guys! Look!

K-ZOO NEWS: Hold it! I'm supposed to interview some dogs. You don't look like a dog!

SLIM: Dog? Dear me, no! You thought we were dogs? No, sir. Not us, sir!

K-ZOO NEWS: Oh. Then could you tell me where the prairie dogs are?

SLIM: Right here, sir. That's us! Right under your nose!

K-ZOO NEWS: But you don't look at all like . . . like *dogs*.

SLIM: Oh, no, sir. Not one bit. Nope, not me! What'd ya expect us to look like?

K-ZOO NEWS: Oh, I don't know. How'd you get the name prairie dog, if you aren't?

SLIM: Well, sir, I think it was you humans which gave it to us. Yes, sir. That's what I think happened, sure 'nough. I hear you call us dogs because of the noises we make. Yes, I believe that's it, all right. We sound like dogs when we talk to each other, see.

K-ZOO NEWS: I see. Well, if you aren't a dog, then what are you?

SLIM: We are what ya call rodents, I think. Have you heard of squirrels? Yes, of course you have. They are some of our closest relatives.

K-ZOO NEWS: I see. Can you tell me about your family?

SLIM: I sure can . . .

(pause)

K-ZOO NEWS: *Will* you please tell me about your family?

SLIM: Oh! Certainly! Yes. We—meaning my wife and our forty-five children—like the wide-open prairie spaces that you find in New Mexico, Arizona, Texas, Colorado, Wyoming, and the Dakotas. (Some of our cousins like to live in the mountains—city life is too much for 'em.) We like company too. Yes, yes. Lots of company! Our "town" has about a thousand inhabitants right now. Yes, sir. We're proud of our town. They call us gra—gri—grog—gregarious! Yes. Gregarious is the word. Yup, that's the word. Means a whole bunch of creatures living together in one area.

K-ZOO NEWS: Interesting! Say, Mr. Prairie Dog, I spoke to some farmers earlier today, and I'm afraid they didn't have too many good words to say about you. What is the deal?

SLIM: Ah, yes! Those ol' farmer boys! We get a real kick out of them. Oh, yes. They're real knee slappers. Them farmers get frantic when they see the pastures turn into prairie-dog towns. You see, our holes, where we live—which you passed off as tiny volcanoes—go down into the ground about fifteen feet or more and then level off into passages and corridors under the ground. And boy, oh boy, when you get horses or cows runnin' through a town of ours, you see a few broken legs, you do. Yes, sir!

K-ZOO NEWS: It does look rather dangerous with all those holes! So what do the farmers do about it?

SLIM: Well, I'll tell ya', mister. They just kill us off, they do. At the turn of the century (that is, in the 1800s), we used to own the West. That's right, own! We did! We used to have entire underground cities! Yes, cities—not just towns! A single one in Texas, the place known for having the biggest of everything, covered 25,000 square miles! Almost 400 million of us lived there. You betcha. I can remember my grandfather, rest his soul, tellin' me about those golden years. But with the farmers gettin' angry at us and killin' us off and all because they couldn't raise their precious cattle, our numbers have really dropped. Yes, they have. A sad thing.

K-ZOO NEWS: Yes, they tell me that you guys can really make it treacherous for cattle and horses. They also tell me that you little fellows can eat up a storm.

SLIM: Oh, do they? Is that what they say? Oh, yes, yes. I do suppose that's true. We eat vegetables, grains, pasture plants, and even insects. Yes, sir, we prairie dogs can really munch down, we can! Some of the farmers who are keepin' track have figured that thirty-two of us can eat as much as one sheep would, or 256 of us will eat as much as a cow (imagine 400 million)!

K-ZOO NEWS: Well, I guess that kind of an appetite would tend to leave very little pasture for cows! Don't you have any other enemies, besides farmers?

SLIM: Yes, we do. We have plenty of vermin after us! Nasty coyotes, hawks, owls, and eagles are after us all the time.

K-ZOO NEWS: Tell me about your town.

SLIM: OK, all right! I'll do that, I will. Let's see here. What do we have? In each town, separate groups rule their own precincts—a precinct is a certain set-off area. Members of a precinct kiss and groom each other and are allowed equal grazing rights. Yes, sir, very organized, it is. Precinct members help each other dig homes. We are tolerant of prairie dogs who are too young to know better and accidentally wander into our precinct. But we stand for no nonsense from older dogs. We chase them out, we do! We watch out for intruders!

K-ZOO NEWS: What happens when an intruder or enemy is near?

SLIM: We warn everyone, of course! What else is there to do? We fling ourselves upright and yelp as loud as we can. Young prairie dogs sometimes fall over backward trying to bark! Very funny, oh, yes, very funny indeed!

K-ZOO NEWS: You look like a young dog. How old are you?

SLIM: Me? I'm three years old today! Yes, sir. Today's my birthday! How 'bout that! I'm touched that you remembered. Yes, sir. I reach middle age today.

K-ZOO NEWS: Well, happy birthday! And thank you so much for this most informative interview! This is your reporter in the middle of hundreds of prairie dogs. Stay tuned for more animal information after this pause for a word from our sponsors.

Crazy Critter

K-ZOO NEWS: Hello again, and greetings from Australia. For three days and nights I've searched muddy streams and lakes, hacked my way through vines, and shared my sleeping quarters with mosquitoes. I still haven't caught a glimpse or sniffed a whiff of my elusive interviewee.

ABERCROMBY: Well, well, well. What's this I find. Hmmm. It looks rather tall, stands on two legs, needs a bath, and smells terrible. Must be an interviewer! I've heard of creatures like you.

K-ZOO NEWS: Uh—thank you, I think, for that flattering introduction! You must be the poisonous, duckbilled, egg-laying Australian mammal I've been sent to interview.

ABERCROMBY: Hmmm. Fairly accurate description. Yes. That sounds like me all right.

K-ZOO NEWS: Oh, good! Could you tell me a little about yourself?

ABERCROMBY: OK. Let's see. Where should I start?

K-ZOO NEWS: How about at the beginning?

ABERCROMBY: At the beginning, huh? OK. We have a bill like a duck's at our beginning. It pretty much stays at the front end of our two-foot body. We use it for finding food underwater. We have soft, thick, yellowish to dark-brown fur that protects us when we're in the water. And we have claws on all four webbed feet, which we use for digging tunnels into the sides of stream beds. Our six-inch tail, which we use as a rudder, is about one-fourth the length of our body. Very useful thing, the tail. Aren't you an odd one! What happened to yours?

K-ZOO NEWS: My tail? Well, I must have lost it somewhere along the way. Now. Back to the subject. From the sound of it, you're more of a bird than anything else.

ABERCROMBY: From what I've told you, it does seem that way. And to make it even worse, we lay eggs!

K-ZOO NEWS: But I thought mammals' young were born alive, not hatched.

ABERCROMBY: Fooled ya, didn't I? The female digs a tunnel in the ground and hollows out a small room at the end. Then she lines the room with leaves and lays her eggs there. The only other egg-laying mammal is the spiny anteater. It lives in Australia too. Don't you wish you lived in Australia with all the *neat* animals?

K-ZOO NEWS: That would certainly be interesting! So, what makes you a mammal then?

ABERCROMBY: We nurse our young with milk. That's the main link between the platypus and other mammals.

K-ZOO NEWS: I understand you are poisonous. Is this true, or is it just a venomous lie?

ABERCROMBY: It's true, all right. We have a spur on each of our back legs. Would you like to have a look?

K-ZOO NEWS: Uh, no thanks. I'll just listen.

ABERCROMBY: I'm hurt! Anyway, the spur is connected to a poison gland. We can poison our enemies with a slash of our foot, and they wonder what's hit 'em. We are the only poisonous mammal in existence, although there are some mammals, I understand, whose saliva is toxic. The poison of the platypus, however, is extremely painful to people.

One wise guy got too close for my liking. I spurred him. He fell to the ground, writhing in pain. I just trotted off in the other direction, unharmed. I got him on his arm. It swelled up very nicely. They tell me he suffered for months from the poison in his system. I guess he even lost control of his wounded hand for some time afterward. Male and female platypuses have the spurs, but the female loses hers before she becomes an adult.

K-ZOO NEWS: Are other platypuses affected by the poison?

ABERCROMBY: Oh, yes! One male got upset with his wife and gave her a swipe with his foot. She almost died!

K-ZOO NEWS: Why don't we switch to another subject? What do you eat?

ABERCROMBY: We dive to the bottom of a stream and scoop up shellfish, shrimp, worms, and all sorts of insects with our bills. We also swallow lots of mud in the process. We weigh anywhere from one to four-and-a-half pounds, and we can eat our weight in food every day!

K-ZOO NEWS: Why haven't I seen any of your relatives in the United States?

ABERCROMBY: We like it here in Australia and Tasmania. We've been removed from our home range only a few times and, believe me, that wasn't our choice. The first captive platypus got fed up with things in the Bronx Zoo in New York and escaped after forty-eight days. Feeding us seems to be a bit more than the zoo people expected at first. One feeder had to spend six hours a day digging for two pounds of earthworms and other delectable goodies for five platypuses. Later, when only one platypus remained, the zookeeper was rudely awakened to the fact that one platypus, all by itself, could eat the same amount as five! Other keepers complained about the amount that had to be provided for a platypus—a half-pound of earthworms, forty shrimp, and forty grubs! And that was only enough for breakfast! In one day, a single platypus can easily devour 540 earthworms, twenty to thirty shrimp, 200 beetle larvae, two small eggs, and two small frogs for dessert.

K-ZOO NEWS: Wow! You really dig in! You have got to be the most bizarre creature on earth!

ABERCROMBY: Well, that's what the European scientists thought when they first saw a platypus in 1797. They were dead sure that it was a big hoax. They figured that someone had carefully sewn the bill of a duck to the body and tail of a beaver, with a few parts of other animals thrown in for good measure.

K-ZOO NEWS: If some of our readers still aren't sure what a platypus is, try this definition: A ravenous, four-and-a-half-pound furry, duckbilled, web-footed, venomous, aquatic, egg-laying mammal!

ABERCROMBY: Couldn't have said it better myself!

K-ZOO NEWS: Thank you, sir, for the interview. This is your faithful reporter, signing off until next time.

Life Otter Be Fun!

K-ZOO NEWS: The boss said I oughta do another interview and sent me to this river. But I don't know what I'm looking for. The boss just said "oughta."

OZZIE: What's that? Whoa, now! This sounds like fun! An interview? Oh, boy! Hey guys, look! A real live interviewer. What fun! I'm an otter—that's what your boss said. I'm sure it is. Can we start, huh, can we? Please, please can we?

K-ZOO NEWS: Uh, sure.

OZZIE: Where do I start, huh? How about fishing? Yeah, fishing is lots of fun. Otters just love fishing, don't we, boys? Swimming around in rivers and streams and lakes. Lots of fun. Chasing trout and other otter fodder. Actually, we river otters aren't particular about what we eat. We'll eat fish, crabs, crayfish, frogs, eggs, insects, snakes, and even water birds and small mammals. We'll eat fish right there in the water, but we take the big ones out to shore, where we can sit down and really enjoy 'em.

K-ZOO NEWS: What about the sea otters? What do they eat?

OZZIE: Now the sea otter is a bit different. He lives along the rocky Pacific coasts of North America and Asia. He lives mainly in the ocean, feasting on sea urchins, crabs, clams, mussels, squid, octopuses, fish, and abalone. The sea otter is quite a clever fellow when it comes to eating

clams. When he finds a clam, he'll bring a rock up from under water. Then he flips over on his back, where he floats with his meal on his belly. Then he smashes the clam against the rock over and over until the clam bursts open. After he eats, he rolls over in the water to wash the bits of shell and food off his fur.

K-ZOO NEWS: You guys must be pretty good swimmers.

OZZIE: Pretty good swimmers?! Ha! Did you hear that, guys? Pretty good swimmers. We're great! We can stay under water for three to four minutes. We can glide through the water without making a ripple! Water is so much fun. We turn somersaults, swim on our backs or our sides, chase each other all over the place, and even dive for pebbles. And do we ever have fun with those boring beavers! Sometimes we swim up to one of them and give his flat tail a good tug and then swim off. No play in them at all, but it's still great sport to tease one. I think otters were made for swimming. I mean, look at these feet, will you? That's right—webbed feet. Excellent for swimming. We have long, sleek bodies—streamlined for stream speed. We flex our bodies up and down, paddle with our hind feet, swish our powerful tails, and zip through the water mighty fast indeed. We have muscles that close our noses and ears tightly so water doesn't get in.

K-ZOO NEWS: But isn't the water cold in the winter?

OZZIE: Oh, I guess so. But we hardly notice. We have special guard hairs that cover and protect our short, thick underfur—sort of like long johns. The underfur traps air and keeps our skin dry. In order for this to work, though, we have to keep our fur clean. So we groom our fur by nibbling at our coat with our teeth and pressing it with our paws. If we get cold, we sometimes soak up some sun when we lie out on the rocks during the day. But that gets pretty boring, just sitting there not moving.

K-ZOO NEWS: It sounds like you're moving most of the time.

OZZIE: Well, sure! If you aren't moving, how can you have fun? Life will just pass you by. That's no fun! And life otter be fun, you know.

K-ZOO NEWS: If you guys are always moving, how come I never see any otters?

OZZIE: Oh, that's part of the fun—keeping out of sight of people. Otters are very discreet. We keep a constant watch, and at the first sign of any disturbance, we take off for the water. An otter, or even an otter family (though otters usually live alone), may be living by a stream or riverbank and go completely unnoticed for years. Otters will often have underwater entrances to their underground den, where they live. So we can come and go without being noticed, even when people are about. But when no one is around, we have a ball sliding down muddy stream banks in summer and icy slopes in the winter. Great fun!

K-ZOO NEWS: Do otters grow very big?

OZZIE: Well, the giant otter can grow to be six feet long, but most otters grow to be three or four feet long, including the tail, which may be twelve to eighteen inches long. We have short legs, so we look awkward when we walk on land. We move quickly enough, but we arch our backs and trot along with an awkward gait. But let us near water and—

K-ZOO NEWS: Yes, yes, of course. Well, I otter—uh—oughta be going now. So long!

Mr. P of the Cat World

K-ZOO NEWS: Well, here we are again. This time I think there's really been a mix-up. I don't mean to complain, but I've been sent all the way to Brazil in search of a—a *puddy tat*! Now, I would have thought a local pet shop would have been a bit more convenient and certainly a much less expensive place to interview a little fur ball!

PAMBELE: A fur ball?

K-ZOO NEWS: Yes, a fur ball. A ten-pound, antisocial—er—uh—

PAMBELE: You were saying something?

K-ZOO NEWS: Uh—

PAMBELE: That's what I thought you were saying. Well, I have half a mind to have you for dinner.

K-ZOO NEWS: Yes, well, um—are you the—the—

PAMBELE: The what? Don't stop now! You're on a roll. What's the matter? Cat got your tongue?

K-ZOO NEWS: Are you my interview? You're a—a—jaguar?

PAMBELE: I prefer being called the American leopard, but (bite my tongue) since you're *such* a nice guy, I'll let you get by with jaguar.

K-ZOO NEWS: Thank you, sir. You're much too kind and certainly much more than ten pounds. Could I ask why you're called the *American* leopard? I mean, this is Brazil, isn't it?

PAMBELE: Hmmm. You must be from the United States. A common mistake that people from the U.S. make is in thinking that America means the U.S. Well, America makes up all this land, which includes South America and Latin America as well as North America. The American leopard lives in several parts of America. In South America, we inhabit parts of Brazil and Paraguay. In North America, we used to occupy Texas, New Mexico, and Arizona. We try to stay clear of there now. You see, the last North American jaguar was killed in 1949 in Arizona.

K-ZOO NEWS: Why were the North Americans so dead set against you? That just kills me!

PAMBELE: It killed us too! I guess you could say the North Americans had trouble with our diet.

K-ZOO NEWS: Your diet?

PAMBELE: Yes. You see, jaguars are quite fond of dining on farmers' horses, cattle, sheep, and pigs. And I guess those folks didn't take too kindly to our culinary pursuits and slaughtered us unmercifully. Even to this day, jags are still hunted and butchered for their spotted skins. We're now an endangered species because of the mass killings, and in these modern times my species has learned to avoid men with guns. We rely on humans to help protect us; but frankly, as long as men are after our skins, we're going to be out on a limb. (Pun intended!) After all, can a leopard change its spots?!

K-ZOO NEWS: I'm sorry about the spots. Have you tried spot remover? Or maybe a little dab of Wite-Out here or there? No, no. Just kidding.

PAMBELE: Not funny!

K-ZOO NEWS: No. No, of course not. A thousand pardons.

So, what do you eat now that horses, sheep, and pigs have been deleted from the menu?

PAMBELE: Interviewers.

K-ZOO NEWS: Pardon me?

PAMBELE: Just getting even. Actually, we have a most stunning diet. It's got to be a diet of large proportions since we are animals of large proportions! You should try to nourish a 400-pound, eight-foot-six-inch body (counting my tail)! Our diet, you ask? Well, we never pass up the chance of making dinner out of a monkey or two. Monkeys are quite annoying little creatures, really. They're always chattering away up in the tops of trees. It's quite bothersome.

K-ZOO NEWS: So you *eat* them? How revolting!

PAMBELE: You think so, huh? And just what exactly would you do?

K-ZOO NEWS: Well—I really couldn't say.

PAMBELE: Thought so. Not really in a position to accuse then, are you? Besides, we don't eat just monkeys. We're not against feasting on deer, and we enjoy filling up on a feathered fowl every now and then. Sometimes, we'll grab an eight-foot alligator and nibble on that for a few days. And fish! We are very fond of fish. We'll lie in wait for a gleaming dinner to swim by, and then *zip*! We snatch 'em! With a flash of a paw and a little luck, we scoop a scaly meal out of the water, pop it in our mouths, and wait for another unsuspecting seafood morsel to float by. An expert fisher jag will sometimes find a branch overhanging a river and stretch out on that to wait.

K-ZOO NEWS: You make it sound so easy!

PAMBELE: Oh my, no! If we aren't catching fish, we're pursuing our prey through almost solid vegetation, up into the tops of trees, and even into water! I guess you could say that we like fast food.

K-ZOO NEWS: A real comedian, aren't you?

PAMBELE: Sorry, I just couldn't resist. Anyway, hunting takes up a great deal of our time (no time for television). We will often swim across large bodies of water in order to reach a different territory or to hunt on an island.

K-ZOO NEWS: I don't get it. You said earlier that you sometimes pursue your prey into the water, and now you're saying you'll swim across wide stretches of water to islands? I thought cats didn't like water.

PAMBELE: Well, I guess jaguars are exceptions (after all, we are exceptional). We love water. We bathe frequently and are excellent swimmers.

K-ZOO NEWS: Say, while we're on the subject of liquid, I've heard that you cats get drunk on occasion.

PAMBELE: Well, yes, in a matter of speaking. It's actually not a drinking problem so much as a food-addiction problem. You see, jaguars, ruthless predators that we are, will search out an innocent avocado tree and (this is so embarrassing) will sit at its base, feasting on the fruit that's fallen to the ground. Very ripe avocado pears will send a jag into raptures. It's simply bliss for us. I'm sure those trees must be descended from the tree of life!

K-ZOO NEWS Fascinating!

PAMBELE: Actually, the American leopard's absolute favorite food is (my teeth tingle at the thought) fresh sea turtles. I'd *kill* for a sea turtle. Have you ever tried sea turtle?

K-ZOO NEWS: Well, no. Can't say that I have.

PAMBELE: You simply must try some!

K-ZOO NEWS: I see. Umm, shall we switch to another topic?

PAMBELE: Yes, I suppose we'd better. I'm getting hungry, and there isn't an avocado tree or sea turtle in sight.

K-ZOO NEWS: You have a family?

PAMBELE: Yes, yes, of course. Silly of me not to have mentioned it earlier! Unlike many animals, the jaguar mates for life. Life is about twenty-two years for a jaguar in the wild. We mate once a year, and the kids arrive a hundred or so days later. Darling little things when they're born!

K-ZOO NEWS: I can imagine!

PAMBELE: When the little tykes are born, they weigh only twenty-four to thirty-five ounces! When they're grown, they'll weigh as much as 400 pounds and measure anywhere from six to seven-and-a-half feet long. They'll stand between twenty-eight to thirty-two inches tall at the shoulder.

K-ZOO NEWS: There are two things most cats are known for—their eyes and their climbing ability. Does that go for you jaguars too?

PAMBELE: Let me tell you about cats' eyes. Our eyes are six times more sensitive to the blue end of the light spectrum than the human eye. That means we can see better at night. Our eyes also adjust much more rapidly to darkness than the human eye does.

K-ZOO NEWS: Why do cats' eyes shine?

PAMBELE: Well, our eyes are covered with a layer of highly reflective cells. This layer collects light from dim light sources. This helps us see better at night also. That layer is what causes a cat's eyes to glow when light hits them.

K-ZOO NEWS: And how about climbing? Are cats good tree climbers?

PAMBELE: Good climbers? Listen! Asia's clouded leopards actually do their hunting in the treetops, they're such good climbers! They can run down tree trunks headfirst! The Latin-American margay also descends trees headfirst, but in a spiraling motion. If he's in a hurry, he'll simply leap to the forest floor. No problem! Both of these cats can actually hang from tree limbs by the claws of one paw. One leopard, weighing only 130 pounds, dragged a 200-pound giraffe up into a tree for safekeeping and fed on it for several days!

K-ZOO NEWS: Well, this has certainly been an enlightening interview. Thank you, sir!

PAMBELE: Don't mention it.

K-ZOO NEWS: This completes the interview. Until next time!

Tern Style

K-ZOO NEWS: This assignment is for the birds! I'm in the frigid northern regions of Greenland, not far from the North Pole. Hmmm, I wonder where the bird I'm supposed to interview is. Oh, maybe that's him over there. Excuse me, are you a cold bird?

ART: No, but I am an Arctic tern.

K-ZOO NEWS: Well, the Arctic is cold, and a tern is a bird, right? So you must be a cold bird!

ART: Look, mister. I don't like your attitude. I'm a very busy bird. I'm getting ready for a 10,000-mile trip, and I haven't even packed yet, so if you could keep it short, I'd be mighty grateful.

K-ZOO NEWS: Did you say a 10,000-mile trip? When the boss said you were a world traveler, he wasn't kidding!

ART: Yes. You see, my summer home is in the north, and my winter home is in the south. You've heard it said, some like it hot, and some like it cold. Well, Arctic terns like it cold and colder. I have friends who have summer homes in northern Alaska, in northern Manitoba, Canada, and in the Arctic regions of Europe and Asia. Most of us spend our winters in the Antarctic Ocean area. The round trip between my two homes is about 20,000 miles.

K-ZOO NEWS: Wow! That's incredible. If I were to drive that far at sixty miles an hour, it would take 333 hours, if I didn't stop on the way! Say, they tell me you spend most of your time in the sun.

ART: True. For eight months of the year the sun never sets where I live. That's twenty-four hours of light for 240 days in a row! We see the sun at midnight—that's why they call this the land of the "midnight sun." Brilliant, huh? For the other four months, the days are always longer than the nights. We see more of the sun than any other living creature on the earth!

K-ZOO NEWS: Well, you certainly are a colorful bird!

ART: Yes, I wear a black cap with tails—a white tail, to be precise. My bill is slender and red. My throat and belly are white, and I have gray wings and bright red feet.

K-ZOO NEWS: Tell me about your kids.

ART: I have two children that entered the world after my wife and I sat on them for twenty-one days.

K-ZOO NEWS: You sat on your children?

ART: Of course! Most birds sit on their eggs, you know. There's Junior 1 and Junior 2 right over there.

K-ZOO NEWS: Over where?

ART: Right there in front of you. Can't you see them?

K-ZOO NEWS: No. I don't see a thing.

ART: Good. That's the whole point. The chicks are covered with down that blends in perfectly with our surroundings. It's hard to believe that those two will be able to fly by the time they're three weeks old! They'll grow to be about seventeen inches long, including their eight-inch tail (with a five-inch fork) and the beak that's just slightly more than an inch long. They'll have a wingspan of about two-and-a-half feet.

K-ZOO NEWS: Wow! What do you have to do to get them to grow like that?

ART: Feed them.

K-ZOO NEWS: I see.

ART: Well, you might see them eventually, if you hang around long enough.

K-ZOO NEWS: Yes. So what do your kids eat?

ART: We feed them mostly small fish and other bite-sized animals that we pick up on the surface of the water. We just grab some food while we're flying over the waves.

K-ZOO NEWS: Sounds like sort of a dive-in for birds on the fly, huh? Where is your nest, anyway?

ART: Well, that's it right under your nose.

K-ZOO NEWS: That's a nest? I thought it was a pile of sticks and seaweed that had washed up on the shore.

ART: Well, who has time to build a condominium when he has to travel 10,000 miles between his summer and winter homes? Didn't think about that, did you? I use what I can find—a few twigs and a bit of grass, with a touch of seaweed to make it homey. I know some terns that just scrape a little dent in the sand or pebbles and call that home. My place isn't so bad.

K-ZOO NEWS: No, you're right. I apologize. As long as your wife and kids are happy.

ART: And they are, thank you.

K-ZOO NEWS: Well, I must fly. Thanks for the interview.

ART: Sure. Guess I'll "tern" in for the night. I've got a long flight ahead of me. Oh, don't step on my children as you're leaving.

K-ZOO NEWS: No, of course not. Say, how do I get outta here?

ART: Well, I always take the first right after the huge iceberg on the left and head due south for about 5,000 miles, then hang a left and keep going . . .

Desert Ship

K-ZOO NEWS: Hello, there! I'm in the middle of the Middle East, here in the hot, hot Arabian desert. I came here to find a ship, but so far all I've seen are mirages, camels, and sandstorms. You might think I'm crazy to be looking for a ship in the desert, where there's no water! Here comes a camel. I'll just ask him if I've missed the boat. Excuse me. Do you know where I could find the ship of the desert?

ALABABA: You've found it!

K-ZOO NEWS: Where?!

ALABABA: Me! Arabian camels have been nicknamed the ships of the desert.

K-ZOO NEWS: Why?

ALABABA: I guess because we're the most efficient method of transportation across the scorching deserts of Arabia. The Bedouins, the desert nomads, use us as they roam the sandy wastelands with their herds of sheep. Bedouins eat barley, millet, and dates, and top this off with camel milk. Until the Bedouins discovered oil in the desert, camels were basically the only mode of transport they knew. Before the oil discoveries, some had never seen a wheel, never mind a car or airplane!

K-ZOO NEWS: I was told that you are one of the oddest mammals alive.

ALABABA: Oh, really? Oddest mammal alive, huh? I don't like to be self-centered or anything, but we are very useful animals.

K-ZOO NEWS: Useful? In what ways?

ALABABA: Well, you already know that the Bedouins drink our milk.

K-ZOO NEWS: That's a start. What else?

ALABABA: No other animal can cope with desert circumstances better than we. Camels just trot on through the hostile elements. Neither heat nor sun nor sand nor dehydration will stop us!

K-ZOO NEWS: You don't mind the heat? Man, it must be over 100 degrees out here!

ALABABA: You underestimate the desert. It's not uncommon to reach 111 degrees Fahrenheit, and sometimes as much as 130 degrees Fahrenheit!

K-ZOO NEWS: So how can you stand it?

ALABABA: It's the shape we're in.

K-ZOO NEWS: You mean you exercise a lot?

ALABABA: No, that's not what I mean. The shape of our bodies prevents overheating. Our long neck and body give us a large surface area relative to how big we are. Somehow this keeps us from getting too hot. Only the more brilliant scientists have attempted to explain how this helps, so I won't go into it.

K-ZOO NEWS: Hmmm. Sounds pretty good to me. But how does that make you useful?

ALABABA: Let me put it this way. Can you walk fifty miles in a day under a scorching sun? No? Camels can.

K-ZOO NEWS: Yes, but I don't see any water around! Maybe you can take the heat, but don't you have a drinking problem?

ALABABA: No problem! We just drink to our heart's content before we set out, and then we can travel for days without water!

K-ZOO NEWS: Days? Come on! Be serious.

ALABABA: Really! One male camel, with his back piled high with packages, traveled for five days without water! When he did get to the next oasis, he drank twenty-five gallons of water in one shot. (That's about 250 drinks from a normal twelve-ounce drinking glass!) A female who was nursing her baby traveled for seven days without water. When she came to an oasis, she greedily took in twenty-three gallons, and then later the same day drank another thirteen gallons!

K-ZOO NEWS: Whew! That's incredible. But there are always a few animals in every species that can run faster or go farther than the rest. I mean, not all camels can go that long, can they?

ALABABA: Let me put it this way. On one fifteen-gallon drink, we camels can travel thirty miles a day for three to four days. And we do that while toting 600 pounds of goodies on our backs. If we don't have to travel quite as far each day, we can go for six to ten days with 1,000 pounds on our backs (one-half a ton)! And all that weight is in addition to our own weight of up to another 1,500 pounds! I suppose you could say we carry a lot of weight.

K-ZOO NEWS: This camel even has a sense of humor! You do sound useful. But how fast can you go?

ALABABA: Granted, we can't move as fast as a car, but then a car can't travel across a sandy desert very easily either. We often travel between five and ten miles per hour.

K-ZOO NEWS: Not bad, compared to a man with 1,000 pounds on his back. How long can a person expect to have a camel around?

ALABABA: We've been known to live as long as fifty-five years. But it's always sad for a mother camel to lose a young one to disease or even to be separated from it. She may mourn the loss of a baby for as long as three months.

K-ZOO NEWS: What do you eat?

ALABABA: It's a simple diet. We eat all sorts of vegetables, which is more than I can say for many humans. We eat a fairly large amount of them, too, considering we have to fill a seven-foot frame.

K-ZOO NEWS: It's a shame you live mainly in the Sahara desert and Arabia. We have some pretty barren land in other parts of the world, too, that you could help out in.

ALABABA: Actually, there have been several attempts to introduce camels into the southwestern United States, Australia, and southern Europe. For some reason the attempts didn't work out very well, so we've just stayed here.

K-ZOO NEWS: Well, sir, you've sold me. I think I'll go out and buy a camel for myself! This is K-ZOO News signing off until next time.

Crazy Mixed-up Bird

K-ZOO NEWS: Wow! I'm off to find the mysterious apteryx, which hides in the deep forests of New Zealand during the day, coming out to hunt only at night. The apteryx is almost invisible, I'm told. I wonder what an apteryx looks like? Sounds like some kind of prehistoric dinosaur. Maybe it's related to the *Tyrannosaurus rex*.

KRAMDEN: No.

K-ZOO NEWS: No? Oh. I was just wondering because . . . uh . . . uh . . . who said that?

KRAMDEN: I did.

K-ZOO NEWS: Where are you, "I did"?

KRAMDEN: Behind you.

K-ZOO NEWS: Oh! Why, you're a kiwi! You can't be the mysterious apteryx!

KRAMDEN: Can't I? Oh, dear. I'm so disappointed. And all my life I've thought I was an apteryx! What a terrible disillusionment!

K-ZOO NEWS: Are you the mysterious apteryx?

KRAMDEN: Yes, of course. What did you expect?

K-ZOO NEWS: Well . . . I don't know. How did you get the names *kiwi* and *apteryx*? Those are strange names for a bird.

KRAMDEN: We got the name *kiwi* from the sound of our call, which sounds like our name—*kee wee, kee wee.*

K-ZOO NEWS: *Apteryx* means "no wings."

KRAMDEN: It's really not an accurate description, though. I do have wings. It's just that I can't see them. They're only two inches long and not particularly useful. Our wings are a real letdown when it comes to flying. I can't even get off the ground with the things!

K-ZOO NEWS: Really! So what do you do?

KRAMDEN: Well, I use my feet, naturally.

K-ZOO NEWS: They're huge!

KRAMDEN: Thank you! Yes, they're very big and very useful for going places. We have short legs with our enormous feet at the end. And we have long claws on our toes. Kiwis are swift runners with huge thighs and well-developed leg muscles.

K-ZOO NEWS: You're a bird, right? So where are your feathers?

KRAMDEN: Yes, I am a bird, and you're looking at my feathers. More like hair than feathers, really. Our feathers don't have the long shaft that make other birds' wings and feathers strong, so our feathers are soft and limp. It gives us the ruffled look—sort of how your father looks when he gets up in the morning and hasn't combed his hair yet.

K-ZOO NEWS: My father's bald.

KRAMDEN: Oh? Well, you're out of luck, then, because he hasn't any hair to ruffle, has he?

K-ZOO NEWS: No. How about your eyes? They're awfully small.

KRAMDEN: Yeah, we can hardly see a thing. If they had glasses for birds, kiwis would need them. Our eyes are about as much good as our wings.

K-ZOO NEWS: I see.

KRAMDEN: You needn't rub it in.

K-ZOO NEWS: No, I meant—oh, never mind. So if you can't see, how do you get around?

KRAMDEN: We follow our noses! We usually go out at night to hunt such food as earthworms, insects, and berries (fallen berries, of course, because we can't fly to get the berries higher up). Our beak is probably our strangest possession. Our nostrils are located at the very tip of our beak—which is quite remarkable, you know. All other birds' nostrils are at the base of their beaks, near their heads. Our beak is long, about half a foot, slightly curved, and it is flexible.

K-ZOO NEWS: A bending beak that doesn't break?

KRAMDEN: Yup! But that's not all. A kiwi beak is covered with a membrane supplied with nerves, which means we can feel our way around with our beaks. We stick our noses into everything. We also have a mustache. The base of our beaks is surrounded with thick hairs. This mustache helps us feel our way around too. We can feel and distinguish among different objects with our beaks.

K-ZOO NEWS: Someone told me you were nearly invisible, but I can see you fine. Was that just a vicious rumor?

KRAMDEN: Well, kiwis are extremely shy birds, who come out mostly at night. Kiwis run and hide whenever anyone comes near. But wouldn't you hide too? I mean, kiwis have been called the "most curious of all birds in existence" and "a roly-poly avian [bird] riddle that waddles on its short legs with the rolling gait of a sailor ashore." And it's been said that the kiwi "looks and acts a bit like an overgrown, above-ground, two-legged mole"!

K-ZOO NEWS: Really? All those things have been said about you? I would have described you as a wig with two legs and a beak.

KRAMDEN: Oh, thanks. I feel much better now.

K-ZOO NEWS: Oh, hey! Don't mention it. Anything else we should know about you?

KRAMDEN: Well, kiwis lay the largest eggs in proportion to our size. Kiwis are about the size of chickens—a little over two feet long and weighing between three and nine pounds. But our eggs are enormous! An eight-pound kiwi may lay an egg that weighs one pound! (That's like a human mother giving birth to a seventeen-pound baby!)

K-ZOO NEWS: You *are* a remarkable bird! Thank you for the interview.

KRAMDEN: You're welcome.

K-ZOO NEWS: Say, you haven't seen any dinosaurs around, have you? I told all my friends I was going to interview a dinosaur.

KRAMDEN: No. Sorry.

K-ZOO NEWS: Ah, that's OK. I was just hoping . . .

Rabbitroos? Kangabits?

K-ZOO NEWS: I'm reporting from down under today, folks, but am I down in the mouth? No, of course not! I'm here in Australia, where the strangest animals in the world hunt and feed and build their homes. My assignment is to find a bandicoot and interview that little marsupial for all it's worth! But I don't see any bandicoots around. I wonder if I'm really in Australia . . . Looks like Australia . . . Maybe if I just call out for a bandicoot, one will hear me. *Bandicoot! Bandico . . .*

RANDY: Shhhhhhh! Quiet, will ya, mate?! We wouldn't want all the Aborigines to hear ya now, would we? If they heard ya, you'd have one of the shortest interviews in your interviewing history, I'll reckon. So pipe down!

K-ZOO NEWS: Uh, sorry. I only wanted to—

RANDY: Yes, yes, of course. Ya meant no harm.

K-ZOO NEWS: You seem kind of secretive. You haven't done anything wrong, have you? You aren't a criminal, are you? An outlaw?

RANDY: Well, no, I don't think so. Nothing that would be considered a criminal bandicoot offense. It's just that Aborigines often take us home for dinner.

K-ZOO NEWS: Really? How thoughtful! Doesn't that save you the trouble of preparing a meal for yourself?

RANDY: Oh, yes! It saves us from ever having to prepare another meal in our lives! When I said the Aborigines take us home for dinner, I didn't mean that they made a meal for us. I meant that *we* made a meal for *them*. You see, Aborigines consider us a delicacy.

K-ZOO NEWS: Oh!

RANDY: Yeah. While a bandicoot is digging its burrow, an Aborigine may happen along on a bandicoot hunt. He puts his ears to the ground and listens for the scratching of the bandicoot digging underground.

K-ZOO NEWS: I'm sorry to hear that . . . I mean, I'm sorry Aborigines hear that. Oh, scratch that . . . I mean . . . uh . . . er . . . So! You live underground?

RANDY: Oh, yes. Some bandicoots dig complex tunnels that spiral wider and wider until the tunnel reaches a hollow chamber that may be as much as six feet underground!

K-ZOO NEWS: Six feet underground? That's cool!

RANDY: Yes, it is cool. Bandicoots spend the hottest part of the day in that hollow chamber.

K-ZOO NEWS: You must be an excellent digger to dig tunnels like that.

RANDY: Well, we aren't bad. In fact, it's been said that some of us bandicoots can rip through ground and dirt with our front feet faster than a man equipped with a shovel and hoe.

K-ZOO NEWS: I don't believe it!

RANDY: Ya wanna race? OK! Ready? Go!

K-ZOO NEWS: No! Wait! Come back up here!

RANDY: Hey, mate, what's the matter? Give up already?

K-ZOO NEWS: I didn't mean that I didn't believe you.

RANDY: That's what ya said.

K-ZOO NEWS: I meant that you're an unbelievably good digger.

RANDY: Oh, yeah, we are. We dig right in. No qualms about getting our feet dirty or getting mud under our fingernails.

K-ZOO NEWS: Speaking of feet, how many toes do you have?

RANDY: Toes? Well, mate, I've got three on my back feet and two on my front feet. And I've got two feet in the back and two in the front. So I would say I've got ten toes. How many toes do you have?

K-ZOO NEWS: Well, let me count . . . uh . . . ten. I have ten too!

RANDY: Wow! We're practically twins.

K-ZOO NEWS: Yeah, but I have ten fingers besides. And I have five toes on each of my feet.

RANDY: So what?

K-ZOO NEWS: Just thought I'd mention it, that's all.

RANDY: Good for you. Now let's change the subject.

K-ZOO NEWS: Certainly. Uh, let's see. Food. If Aborigines eat you, what do you eat?

RANDY: Aborigines or no Aborigines, bandicoots eat insects, tubers, and roots. And sometimes small animals. Often we capture a meal while we're going home. We'll be busy tunneling, and we'll uncover a meal. We dig down so rapidly that the animal doesn't have time to escape.

K-ZOO NEWS: Where do you dig up these meals?

RANDY: Oh, here and there. Fields, gardens—

K-ZOO NEWS: Gardens?

RANDY: Oh, yes. I don't think the gardeners appreciate it very much, though. I think it has something to do with seeing their flowers on the horizontal instead of the vertical. But that seems kind of picky to me. A flower's a flower, right?

K-ZOO NEWS: I see. Say, do you have a pouch like other marsupials do?

RANDY: Oh, sure! But mine's a little different. It opens down and back instead of at the top. I guess we're sort of a rabbit-sized kangaroo.

K-ZOO NEWS: A mix between a rabbit and kangaroo? That would make you a rabbitroo or else a kangabit, wouldn't it?

RANDY: No. It would make me a bandicoot.

K-ZOO NEWS: Yes, of course. I didn't mean to offend you.

RANDY: No, of course not. Bandicoots are sort of a mix of several animals really—rabbits, kangaroos, shrews, elephants—

K-ZOO NEWS: Elephants?

RANDY: Oh, yes. Some bandicoots have trunklike noses.

K-ZOO NEWS: Remarkable! Well, you must have some bandicooting to do, so I won't keep you any longer. Thank you for the interview!

RANDY: No problem! G'day, mate!

K-ZOO NEWS: G'day!

His Bill Holds More . . .

K-ZOO NEWS: The boss said this assignment was for the birds, and he wasn't kidding! I'm a little worried about him, though. He sent me out here to California to find out if there really is a bird with a bill that can hold more than its belly can, a bird that can hold in its beak enough food for a week! I've heard some strange things about Californians, but this is a little beyond bizarre.

BILL: Excuse me, sir. Could I possibly help you? You've been walking around with your mouth open, and it's almost as big as mine.

K-ZOO NEWS: Uh, I don't mean to be rude, but what are you?

BILL: I'm a pelican—a white pelican, to be exact. And I don't mean to be rude either, but what do you want?

K-ZOO NEWS: A pelican! That's it! You've got a big mouth, haven't you?

BILL: Pardon me?

K-ZOO NEWS: Uh—er—let me explain that.

BILL: No need. I get your drift. This pouch on my beak is a whopper, isn't it? It'll hold twelve quarts of water—that's about forty-eight glasses' worth. Actually, my pouch holds two to three times as much as my stomach!

K-ZOO NEWS: So it's true! Your beak *does* hold more than

your belly can! But can it really hold enough food for a week?

BILL: No, that's just a rumor.

K-ZOO NEWS: I've heard several rumors about pelicans. I was told that you feed your young by tearing at your breast and feeding them your own blood.

BILL: Ah, yes. Charming little belief, isn't it? That's an ancient idea that was common in the Middle Ages. I don't know if my ancestors did that back then, but if they did, it's gone out of style, because no pelicans do that now anyway. I think that was just an old legend.

K-ZOO NEWS: I guess that means another rumor I heard is probably just a legend too. I heard that the parent pelicans are eaten by the baby pelicans.

BILL: Oh, really? Well, that can be explained. You see, a parent pelican will carry partly digested fish in its stomach to the baby pelicans. Then the parent passes the food back to the pouch on its bill and lets the young birds plunge their whole beak and head into it and dig around for food. It does look as though the young birds are tearing out the parent's insides.

K-ZOO NEWS: Hmmm, that explains it. How do you catch the fish?

BILL: Well, no one likes to go fishing alone, so a group of us white pelicans gets together and heads for the water. There we get in a semicircle and spread our wings out. Beating our wings scares the fish. We just drive the fish into the shallow water and then shovel them up with our bills. Now the brown pelican works a little differently. He soars way up into the air and flies in a circle until he spots a fish. Then he folds his wings and heads toward the water like a kamikaze dive bomber. He smacks into the water and dives slightly below the surface, popping up with the stunned fish in his beak.

K-ZOO NEWS: You don't get waterlogged?

BILL: Waterlogged? No way! We have large internal stores of air and specially constructed bones that keep us floating.

K-ZOO NEWS: You're a pretty big bird. You must eat a lot.

BILL: Are you suggesting I'm fat? Do you think I need to go on a diet? Is that what you're saying?

K-ZOO NEWS: Well, uh—

BILL: You don't think the ocean is full of low-calorie fish, do ya? "Reduced-calorie tuna"! Not likely!

K-ZOO NEWS: No, of course not. What I meant was—

BILL: Yeah, yeah, I know what you meant. Pelicans are one of the largest birds capable of flight. We eat about four pounds of food a day. A pelican baby needs 150 pounds of fish before it's strong enough for its first flight. Yeah, we are pretty big birds. Sometimes it's a little tough getting off the ground. If there is no wind to help us, we have to run for quite a distance to get up flying speed.

K-ZOO NEWS: Really? All that running just to get airborne?

BILL: It's not easy, you know. We have to get sixteen pounds of feathers, flesh, beak, and bone into the air. That's not easy, even with a wingspan of eight to ten feet.

K-ZOO NEWS: So I suppose you don't fly much?

BILL: Don't fly much? My dear sir! Nothing could be further from the truth! The pelicans that live on the Great Salt Lake in Utah fly thirty to one hundred miles to get to freshwater lakes to eat. There they pick up fish and fly back to feed their young.

K-ZOO NEWS: What about nesting?

BILL: Pelicans usually nest on the ground. We build nests on the shores of islands or even on the shores of inland lakes. We construct a comfortable dwelling place out of earth, gravel, and sand, and complete the structure with twigs on top. Some pelicans live in high-rises. They build a platform in a low tree. I don't care much for heights myself.

K-ZOO NEWS: I don't blame you! Well, this ends another interview with a fascinating bird. His beak truly does hold more than his belly! So long!

Haymakers

K-ZOO NEWS: Well, the boss said I could pick any animal I wanted to interview, and I picked a pika. Hey, there's one now! I think he's whistling at me. That must be the guy I'm supposed to meet. Excuse me . . . Hey, don't run away. Wait!

PETE: Hey, buddy, whaddaya think this is, a hay day or something? Get it? Hay day?

K-ZOO NEWS: Uh, I'm afraid I don't get it.

PETE: Ya don't, huh? Well, I'm Pete the pika, and I guess I'll jus' have to explain it to ya. Ya see, pikas, now, they gotta eat, if ya know what I mean. And seein' I'm a pika, it jus' follows that I gotta eat too, ya know? Well, now, pikas mostly eat just plants an' stuff. Come to think of it, that's all pikas eat. So, we pikas run around all day gatherin' up grass an' the like. Then us pika people take this pika food to a big pika pile, where we pile it. Lotsa *Ps* there, huh? Yes, sir, and our pika pile often gets purty near three feet high, an' sometimes higher! And it's jus' as wide too. Now that's what I call a pika pile!

K-ZOO NEWS: I see what you mean.

PETE: Well, sure ya do! Let me tell ya how it works. Sometimes, we pikas'll live together in groups, like what ya might call families or colonies, and sometimes we live alone. Either together or alone, see? Either way, a pika will go out to cut the grass. We chop some grass off at the root and carry it back to our haystack, or pika pile, and climb on top of that monster and drop off our load o' food.

K-ZOO NEWS: Wait a second! You climb on top of a three-foot-high stack of food?

PETE: You betcha!

K-ZOO NEWS: Now if I've calculated correctly—

PETE: Oh, I'm sure ya' have.

K-ZOO NEWS: —you're only about six inches long. I'm five feet tall, and if I were to climb on top of a pile of food in the same proportion to my size, I'd not only get in trouble, but I'd be thirty feet in the air!

PETE: Well, sure ya would. Dizzying heights! But no matter. Now, as I was sayin', we don't work on our pika pile all the time. No, no. Ya see, as you was probably wonderin', we spend most of our time just eatin' in the spring and early summer.

K-ZOO NEWS: Guess you'd have to in order to get through a pile of food six times as tall as you are.

PETE: Oh, sure, I see your point. Yes, of course. Now, we start workin' on that pika pile come midsummer. Yes, sir, we start pilin' up luscious grasses, herbses, and twigses. We only weigh from six to fourteen ounces (that's about the weight of a roll of quarters), but we gotta pile up the food. Now, I s'pose you're a-wonderin' how come we build up this stack of food right out in the open, where anyone could jus' come along an' dine on it.

K-ZOO NEWS: Well, yes, I was, now that you mention it.

PETE: I'll tell ya what we do. We get a patrol pika, that's what we do. 'Course we do! Now this here patrol pika seeks out a pika perch. That is, he finds a high place to use as a lookout. Now, if this patrol pika sees a pesky thief a-preyin' on our pika pile, he'll let the rest of us know, and we chase it off. And if the patrol pika sees a pika predator come around, such as a hawk or an eagle or maybe even a wicked weasel, the patrol pika lets out a call to let the rest of us pikas know! Then we dive for cover! Wouldn't you?

K-ZOO NEWS: Yes, of course!

PETE: The warnin' sound is quite different for different pikas, of course. Some pikas make a sharp barkin' sound, while other pikas sound like bleatin' lambs. Imagine sounding like some other animal, huh? Jus' about blows your mind, don't it now?

K-ZOO NEWS: Well—

PETE: Yup, I can see it does! I can see you're amazed. Now when it comes wintertime, it gets purty cold where we live and—

K-ZOO NEWS: And where do we—I mean, *you*—live?

PETE: Oh, we live in western North America clear up to Alaska, and we live in the northern parts of Europe and Asia. Some of us live 17,500 feet up in the Himalaya Mountains—that's the highest altitude any mammal can survive at. After that, it's never-never land! But never mind. Where we live, it gets mighty cold in the winter, an' that's the whole purpose of the pika pile. Then when it gets cold and snow drifts all over, coverin' up good food, we jus' have a pika pigout on our pika pile! At least that's how we do it. Some pikas take their harvested grass down into their burrows, and some pikas store the grass between rocks. Now, don't get me wrong! Pikas aren't scared of the cold. We'll go out even if the ol' therm-o-meter reads four degrees Fahrenheit. It's just a bit harder to find food at that time of the year, that's all.

K-ZOO NEWS: Yes, of course.

PETE: Now, I s'pose you'll wanna know about the wife an' kids.

K-ZOO NEWS: Uh . . . that was my next question, of course.

PETE: Well, I'll tell ya, my friend. I met my wife when I was on the rocks. Ya see, when us pikas rub our cheeks against a rock, it leaves a mighty powerful pika perfume that them purty little female pikas can't resist. (It marks off our pika territory, too, but that's beside this here pika point.) I had jus' put on some Pika of Paris perfumatory when along she comes, and I was clean swep' off my feet with this little beauty of a pika. She had the cutest pika ears you've ever seen, and her coat was a purty brownish gray—not like some red-colored ladies I've seen. Well, so far, we've raised thirty young 'uns together.

K-ZOO NEWS: Thirty? You've been married a long time, haven't you?

PETE: Oh, yes, we've been married for two years now. We have anywhere from two to six kids, two or three times a year. Kids are so much fun! Mother an' I hope to be together till we die. Don't think I'll make it more than a few more months, but I have a feelin' Mother will live to a ripe ol' age of three years, an' that's a mighty full life for a pika.

K-ZOO NEWS: Well, thank you for the interview. Until next time . . .

PETE: Oh, sure! It's been great fun! But you really should talk more. I mean, really. You hardly said a thing . . .

Just the Facts

It is two o'clock in the morning, and I am standing in the middle of a field on South Island, part of New Zealand. My assignment? To discover all there is to know about the disappearance of the kakapo. First, I have to find out what a kakapo is. That's why I'm here in the middle of the night. And that brings you up to date on the current situation.

K-ZOO NEWS: Excuse me, ma'am. Do you know what a kakapo is?

KARI: It is a flightless, nocturnal parrot. It can be found only in the . . .

K-ZOO NEWS: Uh, just the facts, ma'am.

KARI: Those are the facts, buddy!

K-ZOO NEWS: Sorry, I've always wanted to say that. Now, when you say nocturnal, what do you mean?

KARI: I mean nocturnal—only comes out after dark. You do know what dark is?

K-ZOO NEWS: Yes, of course. I'm in the dark quite a bit, so I'm familiar with the term. I wonder if you know how many kakapos there are on this island.

KARI: On this island? Why, there are only about 100 kakapos left in the whole world, never mind this island!

K-ZOO NEWS: Hmmm. Interesting. I'll just make a note of

that. Nocturnal bird. Only 100 left in world. But, of course! I see a connection already! If there were only 100 of me left in the world, I wouldn't wander casually about in broad daylight either! But wait! There's only one of me left . . .

KARI: Thank goodness for small blessings.

K-ZOO NEWS: I beg your pardon? Oh, never mind. I need more information, ma'am. Anything you tell me can and will be held against you in a court of law.

KARI: Excuse me?

K-ZOO NEWS: Oh, sorry. I always get mixed up. I meant, anything you can tell me will be a great help. You see, I am looking for the disappearing kakapo, and any information you have—

KARI: What do you think you're talking to, anyway?

K-ZOO NEWS: Well, you look kind of like a green owl.

KARI: Criminals must surely shudder with fear when you're on their track. A green owl? Have you ever heard of a green owl? And how do you explain the way I stand? Have you ever seen an owl that walks like a duck?

K-ZOO NEWS: Please! One question at a time.

KARI: Look, Mr. Sheerluck Holmes, you're looking at a kakapo!

K-ZOO NEWS: You're a kakapo?! I've found the disappearing bird! I'm a hero! The world's greatest sleuth! I amaze myself—

KARI: Pipe down, skippy! Look, let me tell you something about myself, and maybe you'll increase your chances of seeing other kakapos. For one thing, looks can be deceiving. Kakapos are parrots, but other than our beaks and feet, we don't look like your average parrot or macaw.

K-ZOO NEWS: That's good. We need to disguise you! We

need a cover. What's different about you?

KARI: I thought that was fairly obvious, but I'll tell you anyway. Our heads look like an owl's—even have the unique eye markings of an owl. Our posture is upright like a penguin's, instead of parallel to the ground like any other parrot's. And we waddle around like a duck, rather than walk like a parrot. We eat plants such as mosses, leaves, sprouts, berries, and even a few fungi.

Kakapos are the world's heaviest parrots. We are the size of a crow but weigh as much as six pounds. We can't fly like other parrots, but we use our strong clawed feet to climb trees. Kakapos are the world's only flightless parrots.

K-ZOO NEWS: Doesn't that put you at a disadvantage against your enemies?

KARI: You're quick, aren't you?

K-ZOO NEWS: Oh, sure. Doesn't take me long to catch on! I've a mind like a steel trap.

KARI: Yes, I can see that. Until the relatively recent arrival of the Maori people on the islands where the kakapo lives, we really had no natural enemies. Our islands contained no land mammals, except for bats, which weren't a big problem. But when the Maori arrived, three new enemies arrived too: dogs, rats, and humans. The Maori people thought we were a sweet bird.

K-ZOO NEWS: Well, that's good, isn't it?

KARI: Yes—for them! Sweet to eat, I meant.

K-ZOO NEWS: Oh. That's not so good.

KARI: Right again. Your sharp wit must have saved you in many tight situations. Anyway, not only did the people relish our meat, so did the dogs that came with them. And, when the people arrived on ships to our islands, so did rats.

K-ZOO NEWS: But a rat can't eat a six-pound parrot!

KARI: Right again! We aren't born weighing six pounds, you know. The rats find kakapo chicks easy prey.

K-ZOO NEWS: Don't you fight back?

KARI: How? Our only form of defense is to sit still and rely on our camouflage. If we are in a tree and a predator approaches, we instantly drop to the ground without moving our wings, like we've been shot. This makes us easy prey for everyone, including cats, stoats (weasel-like animals), and ferrets. To top it all off, fire, deer, goats, and opossums have destroyed the habitat of low trees and shrubs that was our home and that provided some protection. Many kakapos, of course, were killed by predators, but many were also transported to England as oddities and pets.

K-ZOO NEWS: That must have been awful!

KARI: Well, kakapos are an optimistic lot, and we made the best of a bad situation. The English cherished us as pets and treated us very well, so we returned their affection. I know one of my distant relatives became so fond of the children in his English home that he followed at their heels everywhere they went. Another fellow would sit in the corner of a room, watching his master's hand, then run across the room, seize the hand with his claws and beak, and wrestle with it like a kitten does with a ball of yarn. Kakapos also entertained their masters by demonstrating a sense of humor, like the kakapo who marched through the house with his head twisted between his legs, checking out how things looked upside down. But our natural home is better.

K-ZOO NEWS: I've got it! Why don't you have more children and repopulate the islands?

KARI: Kakapos may breed only twice in ten years instead of yearly, as other parrots do. When a new nest is started, it will contain two to four small, pear-shaped bundles of amazingly white, down-covered chicks. Not all the fledglings survive. Sometimes none survive. Our nests are in holes in the ground instead of in trees, and ground nests are easier for predators to destroy.

K-ZOO NEWS: Is there anything else I should know, ma'am?

KARI: Well, perhaps just one other thing. Kakapos are leks.

K-ZOO NEWS: Oh. Of course. I just took that for granted . . . Uh, what's a lek?

KARI: A lek is one of only thirty kinds of animals in which the males gather at certain spots and make a wonderful display to attract the females—that is to say, they show off, strut their stuff, and grandstand. The male kakapo makes pathways to areas specially prepared for the display. An area of ground is dug out for a stage. At night, a male enters this arena and inflates his chest to an enormous size and heaves it up and down as his head bobs up and down. Accompanying this display is his deep booming call. Each boom seems to involve every muscle in his body. The noise is something like blowing across the top of a large glass bottle. The display lasts all night.

K-ZOO NEWS: Thank you, ma'am. Perhaps I'll see you again as I continue my investigation. Until then . . .

Boomers and Fliers

K-ZOO NEWS: Greetings! This is your friendly news reporter back in Australia and its surrounding islands. I'm standing in a wide-open field, desperately scanning the horizon for a boomer. Hmmm. Here comes someone toward me now. . . . Excuse me, Mr. Kangaroo, have you seen a boomer around this area?

BOOMER: A boomer? As a matter of fact, I have!

K-ZOO NEWS: Great! Could you direct me to him?

BOOMER: Sure! Step two feet in my direction, and you'll be staring one straight in the face!

K-ZOO NEWS: You're a boomer? But—but I thought you were a kangaroo!

BOOMER: There, there now. Don't get so worried and befuddled. Let Uncle Boomer explain. Male kangaroos are called boomers, and female kangaroos are called fliers.

K-ZOO NEWS: Why?

BOOMER: Because, my little interviewer, when kangaroos are faced with an enemy, the females tear off in a random direction, while an older male, like me, stays to fight. We pound the ground with our feet as a warning, and that's how we get the name "boomer." The female gets the name "flier" because she takes off. And when the fliers flee, they really move! Kangaroos will panic at the

sight of a predator and scatter in all directions. It's each one for herself! We're very cautious and don't take any chances.

I'm embarrassed to tell you this, but yesterday the funniest thing happened. Our group was grazing out in the middle of a field when one of the fliers noticed some movement in the grass. That was all they needed, and all the fliers scattered. Later, we found that it was only a little kitten stalking a mouse in the field!

K-ZOO NEWS: Wow! A little kitten caused a whole stampede? Who *are* your enemies?

BOOMER: Our main enemies are dingoes.

K-ZOO NEWS: Please, sir! I know they're your enemies, but let's not start calling them nasty names!

BOOMER: Dear me! You must be from the United States! Dingo *is* the name of our enemy.

K-ZOO NEWS: Oh.

BOOMER: The dingo is a doglike animal that can't seem to get enough kangaroo meat. They come storming into our calmly grazing group of kangaroos and stir up trouble.

K-ZOO NEWS: What do you do to get rid of them?

BOOMER: A male will brace his back against a tree, then kick with his powerful legs at the dingo. Believe me, a dog doesn't stick around long! If one becomes so bold as to jump at our throats, we simply grab it in our arms, hold it to our chest, and pound away on it with powerful slashes of our feet.

K-ZOO NEWS: From the looks of things, I'd say you might have to run quite a distance to some areas before finding a tree. What then?

BOOMER: If there doesn't happen to be a tree around, we grab a dingo and take it into the water. Then we hold it under until it drowns!

K-ZOO NEWS: Wow! You really take control of the situation, don't you?

BOOMER: Well, yes. I guess so.

K-ZOO NEWS: Why do they keep trying?

BOOMER: The dingo's technique is to pick one kangaroo and run it to exhaustion.

K-ZOO NEWS: But I thought kangaroos were great jumpers.

BOOMER: We are! We can reach speeds of fifty miles an hour and can leap in bounds of up to thirty feet! But we can keep up that speed for only a mile or two, and dingoes wear us out if they keep after us.

K-ZOO NEWS: Some claim that kangaroos have jumped eight-foot-high fences, and one writer says a kangaroo hurtled over a pile of logs six feet high and forty feet long. Is this really possible, or are they exaggerated tales?

BOOMER: It could possibly be true. Unfortunately, not all of us are experts at clearing such obstacles. Sometimes a kangaroo can really damage himself when he overestimates his ability to jump a six-foot barbed-wire fence. The results of "almost" making it are not good at all.

K-ZOO NEWS: I can imagine. How tall are you?

BOOMER: Right now I'm six feet tall and weigh ninety pounds, which is average for an adult male. Curiously enough, males continue to grow throughout their life. One old boomer grew to a height of seven feet and weighed 180 pounds! The average female is much smaller. Fliers are usually under four feet and seldom weigh more than fifty pounds.

K-ZOO NEWS: You had mentioned earlier that you graze in groups. How large is a group?

BOOMER: It varies rather widely. A group is generally made up of six to twelve of us. But it is not unusual to find a group of thirty or fifty.

K-ZOO NEWS: I see. What do you graze on?

BOOMER: We aren't picky. We eat what's available.

K-ZOO NEWS: I'm afraid I don't understand.

BOOMER: Let me put it this way. We are vegetarians—grass and herb eaters, to be exact. When we are in a blade-grass area, we eat blade grass. If there happen to be some soft, tender shoots at hand, then we eat those. Really, we aren't choosy eaters and will eat almost any kind of grass out there.

K-ZOO NEWS: Do you have a family?

BOOMER: Oh, yes! I have—hey! Look who's coming! It's my wife!

K-ZOO NEWS: Well, hello there, Mrs. Flier! We were just talking about you! Maybe you could tell us about your family.

MRS. FLIER: Certainly! We have one child—Joey is his name. (As a matter of fact, all baby kangaroos are named Joey!) You should have seen him when he was born! He was terribly cute. He was so small! Knee-high to a grasshopper. He was a pink, helpless little thing. You'd never guess he'd turn out to be a six-foot, ninety-pound giant!

JOEY: Oh, Mom! Quit making such a fuss! Can we go now?

MRS. FLIER: All right, Joey, in a minute. Joey's so high-strung! I'd better take him to play. Nice meeting you, Mr. Interviewer!

K-ZOO NEWS: Oh, why, thank you! Nice meeting you too, Mrs. Flier. 'Bye, Joey! Well, then, Boomer, you must be very proud of your son!

BOOMER: You betcha! Look at him run off to play, kicking daringly at tree stumps. Doesn't give his mother a bit of rest! Look at him now! He's gotten hold of her ears and is kicking at those! He's such a character! Now he's trying to eat the same piece of grass his mother is.

K-ZOO NEWS: Dear me! I think I'd get angry with such a rambunctious and feisty little critter.

BOOMER: Oh, no. Mother is very patient with him. If she gets fed up with his antics, she'll just move out of his reach. It's hard to believe that energy-exuding fur ball was only a bean-shaped object not so long ago. When Joey was born, he weighed only one ounce and was a mere three-fourths of an inch long!

K-ZOO NEWS: Well, thank you for such a *factsinating* interview. This is K-ZOO News signing off until the next exciting feature! Tune in next time. Same time, same place!

Dizzy Des, the Littler Riddler

K-ZOO NEWS: I'm here in the Pyrenees mountains looking for the world's smallest elephant! I expect I'll see him any minute now.

DIZ: Hey, bub!

K-ZOO NEWS: Huh?

DIZ: I said, hey, bub!

K-ZOO NEWS: What on earth are you?

DIZ: Don't matter if I'm on earth, in the water, or in the air—I'm a desman, dude!

K-ZOO NEWS: You mean your name's Desmond?

DIZ: Nah! My name is Dizzy. You asked what I was, not who—and I told you. I'm a desman.

K-ZOO NEWS: Are you the world's smallest elephant? You look like a mole!

DIZ: Mole holes and punk trunks! You think I'm an elephant, do you? Well, I've got a trunk for a nose, but that's as far as it goes—just to the end of my nose, ya' knows? I'm a molelike mammal.

K-ZOO NEWS: Yes, I see your trunk. But what's it do?

DIZ: What's it do, he asks! What's it do? Do?! I'll tell ya' what it do's, dude! It moves in all directions, it does! It snorkels while I swim so I can breathe while I'm under the water there. You see, I don't, so it helps.

K-ZOO NEWS: Huh?

DIZ: I don't see, I say to you. My eyes never open to see the sun that never shines into my world, nor the moon that is always out when I am but never helps me see. I'm only out at night to look for food I cannot see since my eyes never open to see the sun that never . . .

K-ZOO NEWS: Yes, yes. You said that.

DIZ: Oh. Oh-kay!

K-ZOO NEWS: Well, what's that have to do with your trunk?

DIZ: Oh! I see! Actually, I don't see. So my trunk, you see (don't you see?), helps me swim about by feeling my way through the water. I just follow my nose. Since it always goes first, my nose always knows first what's ahead. By using my Jacobson's organ, I can find my way around obstructing obstacles.

K-ZOO NEWS: Your Jacobson's organ?

DIZ: It's not really Jacobson's organ—it's *my* organ, but Jacobson discovered it. It's what scientists call a primitive olfactory structure (that means: an underdeveloped mechanism for smelling) used by fish and amphibians to allow them to smell under underwater circumstances. The scientists tell us that only a few mammal species have this smelly device, but as a desman and a mammal, I have been granted this underdeveloped mechanism for smelling!

K-ZOO NEWS: So you use it to get food?

DIZ: Shore! Wouldn't you, if you were blind? My trunk tracks down food like stone flies, caddis flies, mayflies, and mayfly larvae. It does a good job too! And a good thing it does a good job, since in the winter I eat two times my weight in food every day just to keep warm!

K-ZOO NEWS: And what is your weight?

DIZ: Wait! I'll tell you! Only fifty to eighty golden grams (which is the same weight as fourteen to twenty-three bronze pennies).

K-ZOO NEWS: OK. I can see how your trunk helps you eat, but you can't smell the rocks in the streams you swim in!

DIZ: Smell rocks? I guess I just take rocks for granite (let's make that granted instead of granite). Rocks are hard but not hard to avoid. I use this nose to touch and test and probe every surface by swinging it in a sweeping motion so quickly, my nose would look like a blur to your eyes. With many thousands of tiny hairs on the tip of my nose, it is very sensitive (so please don't offend it). My nose knows differences in roughness that would be rough for a human to tell the differences between.

My trunk is a bag of tricks! By poking it above water, I can breathe when I'm under water. I use it as a tool to dislodge food from the river's bottom and then move the food to my mouth. And I use it to learn about my environment. So it's no surprise that a desman with closed eyes can be taken two miles from his territory and be back home in an hour!

K-ZOO NEWS: But why go back to your old territory?

DIZ: A desman doesn't desert his 200 yards of riverbank. I guard my riverbank like it was Fort Knox! Both sexes fiercely fight for footing along a river. How and when we drop our defenses long enough to get together to mate is classified as classified information.

K-ZOO NEWS: You can't tell me?

DIZ: It's not that I can't, but I won't!

K-ZOO NEWS: What a colorful little character you are!

DIZ: Colorful? You make me sound like a rainbow! I'm not. I've got silvery fur and white fur for my belly, with a red-tipped snout to top it all off. Little? I suppose that I am. My body's half a foot long at the longest. My tail's half a foot, too, but I don't walk on it, and please don't you! Speaking of tails, I'll you the tale of mine (my tail's tale, that is). It has a few hairs hair and there and is covered with scales. At the base of my tail is a large musky scent gland. My enemies have sense not to eat such a thing that has sent such a scent in its path.

I have four feet, with two forefeet that are fringed with stiff hair and partially webbed, while my hind feet are webbed quite completely. I live only in streams in Spain and in France, and only in streams not polluted. I burrow deep burrows on the banks of the water and place all of my doors below water. When rivers turn hard with ice from the cold, it's not hard to get into my burrow below. Our tunnels will tunnel as far as eighteen feet to a dry nesting place near the ground's surface.

K-ZOO NEWS: Well, you certainly rattle on in riddles, but I thank you for the interview.

DIZ: And I think I thank you, though I think it's all through, for this interview with you. Whew!

Is This Fox Fur Real?

K-ZOO NEWS: The boss is giving me the cold shoulder. I asked him what my next assignment was, and he sent me to Siberia! Can you believe it? It must be thirty below zero out here.

OLLIE: No. It's more like thirty-eight below, actually. You forgot wind chill.

K-ZOO NEWS: Yes. Of course. Uh, what are you?

OLLIE: What a strange question. I'm an Arctic fox, of course. You're new here, aren't you?

K-ZOO NEWS: Uh, yes, you could say that. I suppose you've been sent here to Siberia because you're being punished for some hideously criminal act?

OLLIE: No. I live here.

K-ZOO NEWS: What!!?! *Live* here? By choice? Why?

OLLIE: Well, I don't know. I kind of like it, I guess.

K-ZOO NEWS: But there's nothing but miles upon miles of ice and snow.

OLLIE: That's not true. Just over that little hill is a polar bear.

K-ZOO NEWS: A, uh, what?

OLLIE: Oh, never mind. He's harmless enough.

K-ZOO NEWS: But you live here? How do you keep warm?

OLLIE: See this white coat?

K-ZOO NEWS: Yes.

OLLIE: Gorgeous, isn't it? Pure white, fluffy, thick, and very warm. It keeps my short legs, round ears, and short muzzle toasty. This coat gives insulation like you've never dreamed of. It creates a barrier that prevents body heat from escaping as fast. It keeps me comfortable down to negative forty degrees Fahrenheit. After forty below an Arctic fox can raise its metabolism, which means it uses energy to make heat faster than normal. At ninety-five degrees below zero, an Arctic fox would only have to raise its metabolism by thirty-seven percent to feel comfortable.

K-ZOO NEWS: Ninety-five below? I can hardly imagine that.

OLLIE: Let me see if I can help. At that temperature, you'd be dead in less than five minutes.

K-ZOO NEWS: I think I'm getting the picture.

OLLIE: Arctic foxes enjoy the ice world of the north. We roam the tundra and ice in west Greenland and islands in the Bering Sea and North Atlantic Ocean. Some of my friends have gone within twenty-five miles of the North Pole. Some have been closer than that to the "pole of inaccessibility." That's the point in the Arctic Ocean that is farthest from land.

K-ZOO NEWS: How do you get out there?

OLLIE: Walk or hitchhike on icebergs.

K-ZOO NEWS: Walk? I can barely take a step without falling, never mind traveling that far! It must be hundreds of miles!

OLLIE: Well, Arctic foxes do have a bit of an advantage over humans. Our feet are equipped with sharp claws, and the soles of our feet are covered with fur. We can run and dance over the slickest ice without a second thought. During the winter months, when food is hard to find, an Arctic fox will travel as much as a thousand miles.

K-ZOO NEWS: Whew! That's an awful long way for food. What do you eat, anyway?

OLLIE: During the spring and summer, foxes feast on chunky seabirds called dovekies. They are abundant and easy to catch. We also feast on lemmings, which are abundant, too, and as everyone knows, they aren't the world's brainiest rodents. But when the birds fly away during the winter, and the snow falls deep to cover the little lemmings, food is hard to find.

K-ZOO NEWS: What do you do?

OLLIE: Well, during the spring and summer we stash away lots of food. My cache last year consisted of thirty-six dovekies, four snow buntings, and a number of dovekie eggs. That would have lasted me for a month. But the cache is only for an emergency. In the winter, we eat just about anything; from crushed shrimp to fish and frogs and even bumblebees. Sometimes we dig pits into the snow and wait above in ambush for a lemming to appear.

If we're really fortunate foxes, we may find a seal or walrus or a whale washed up on the beach. For a seven-pound fox, a fifty-ton whale is a mountain of food. A fox will actually tunnel into the carcass, and when it gets done, the whale looks more like a giant slice of Swiss cheese than a whale.

Even though we can smell food seven feet below the ice, most foxes are hungry for most of the winter. That's the reason foxes travel so far—to search out food. If it's a really bad winter, a fox will tag along behind a polar bear. Then, when a polar bear finishes eating the blubber from a seal he's killed, we'll eat the rest. Sometimes a fox will go two weeks without a meal. Dieting is no fun.

K-ZOO NEWS: Do you hunt in groups?

OLLIE: Lans, no! If there's one piece of food (say a bumblebee) and two foxes, then fox fur flies—that is to say, war breaks out. The foxes threaten each other by arching their backs and stiffly raising their tails. The rivals growl and snap and then rush toward each other, colliding flank to flank or rump to rump. No, Arctic foxes usually hunt alone.

K-ZOO NEWS: Do you have a family?

OLLIE: Yes. Each year, after winter, the foxes come back to the den where they raised their last litter and prepare to raise a new litter. If food is plentiful, a litter may be as large as twenty-five cubs! A litter that size will eat sixty to one hundred lemmings in a day. If food isn't as abundant, a litter may have only three to five pups, and the parents may hunt fourteen to nineteen hours a day and still not find enough food to feed the pups.

K-ZOO NEWS: What is a fox's den like?

OLLIE: Large and dry with many tunnels. An Arctic fox always digs its den where the den can drain easily to keep it dry. Each year, when the father and mother return from their winter wanderings, they dig a new entrance to the den and add new chambers. Some dens are reused for fifty years and have as many as 100 different entrances, but the average den has only ten entrances.

K-ZOO NEWS: Well, I thank you for the interview. I wonder if you could tell me how to get back to North America?

OLLIE: Sure. Take the first iceberg to the right and float due east until . . .

The Bird That Can't Fly

K-ZOO NEWS: Hello! I'm your friendly news reporter on location in Antarctica, covering a story on the bird that can't fly.

REGINAL: Excuse me?

K-ZOO NEWS: What's wrong?

REGINAL: What's that supposed to mean—"bird that can't fly"?

K-ZOO NEWS: Well, everyone knows penguins can't fly! And you are an Adélie penguin, if I'm not mistaken, sir.

REGINAL: Yes, I'm an Adélie. But what's all this nonsense about my not being able to fly? Penguins can fly! As a matter of fact, we can fly at speeds of more than twenty-five miles an hour. True, we fly underwater, but it's still flying!

K-ZOO NEWS: I see. Well, I stand corrected. Can we get on with the interview now?

REGINAL: Yes, yes. Forgive me for flying off the handle. (No pun intended.) Do go on.

K-ZOO NEWS: Where do you live, sir?

REGINAL: We raise our kids in the Antarctic every September or October. Mother and I come back from vacation about then and search out exactly the same spot in our

territory that we used last year—kind of a winter-home arrangement.

K-ZOO NEWS: Isn't it difficult to find the same place when it might be covered with several feet of snow?

REGINAL: For a human, I imagine it would be quite difficult indeed—it might take a miracle. But it really isn't so hard for us. Last season, it was easy to find our home, since the group of penguins we hang around with had dwindled to an all-time low of about 70,000.

K-ZOO NEWS: They tell me that you are an avid rock collector, Mr. Penguin.

REGINAL: Yes. We Adélie families mark off our territory with small rocks that we collect from the nearby ocean. We place about fifty of them in a circle, and this becomes our territory.

K-ZOO NEWS: How large is your territory?

REGINAL: There's enough space between our pebble circle and our neighbor's pebble circle to ensure that we don't hit each other with our beaks when we turn our heads. We're so fortunate to have found such a lovely, wide-open spot in which to place our circles!

K-ZOO NEWS: I see. Could you tell us about the explorer incident that took place in the Antarctic several years ago?

REGINAL: Ah, yes! Those explorers were such great fun! We had a picnic with them. They set up all sorts of eye-catching objects around our area. Anyway, we penguins decided to see what this was all about. So when the explorers weren't looking, a few of us waddled over to one extremely fascinating instrument and pushed it to see what would happen. I guess it was alive, because it fell over and gave out some kind of cry—of pain or something—and then there was a flash of light. Perhaps we had upset the creature. We saw the explorers coming back, yelling and screaming. I guess they were mad at us for killing their pets. We got out of there pretty fast. After that, they put up a fence so we couldn't visit anymore.

K-ZOO NEWS: Curious little critter, aren't you! Tell me about your family.

REGINAL: We have a rather small family. Let's see, I believe there are about twenty-six members. There's Sean, Wayne, Kari Lou—

K-ZOO NEWS: OK! I get the point already. Let's move on to some other aspect of your family.

REGINAL: Well, we have two kids each season. Mother and I take turns caring for the little ones. One of us will stay home for two weeks with the kids while the other goes off to eat. Then we switch when our partner returns. At the end, I take full responsibility and stay at home for more than three weeks. I lose almost half my weight during that time!

K-ZOO NEWS: I must say I'm impressed! Do you have a picture of your latest children?

REGINAL: Oh, yes! I don't go anywhere without their pictures. Here, take a look.

K-ZOO NEWS: They sure are handsome little fellows. How tall are they?

REGINAL: They'll be anywhere from one to four feet tall when they grow up.

K-ZOO NEWS: Where do all the Adélie penguins get that ring spot around their eye from?

REGINAL: Ahhh! That's a secret! If I told you, everyone would want one!

K-ZOO NEWS: Oh. Well . . . Say, I understand you penguins can stay underwater for up to seven minutes! Is that true?

REGINAL: Yes, it is. And flying at twenty-five miles an hour for seven minutes means I can go almost three miles underwater without taking a breath! I challenge any human to run three miles without breathing! You can't do it!

K-ZOO NEWS: Well, what do you do while you're underwater? Do you have any enemies there?

REGINAL: What we do underwater is fish for our food. As far as enemies, we penguins have many enemies, such as the leopard seal. That's why we are so cautious before going in. Some folks tell a story that makes us Adélies seem rather cruel. They say that we will go to the edge of the ice and line up along its edge without jumping in. Then, we push one of our friends into the water. If he comes to the surface, we all go in, because we know there are no leopard seals about. If the unfortunate fellow doesn't come up, we figure he's been eaten. So we all turn around and walk away—so the story says.

K-ZOO NEWS: Really!? Uh, changing the subject now. It's a bit chilly here in the Antarctic. Aren't you freezing?

REGINAL: I certainly would be if I weren't equipped correctly. I may not have a thick fur coat, but under these feathers is a half-inch of blubber! That keeps me pretty toasty, even when the 100-mile-an-hour winds make the usual forty degrees below zero seem even colder.

K-ZOO NEWS: Well, thank you for your time and for such an interesting story.

REGINAL: Certainly, sir.

K-ZOO NEWS: This is your K-ZOO News reporter, reporting from the home of all Adélie penguins—the Antarctic. Stay tuned for more news right after this . . .

No Big Deal

K-ZOO NEWS: The boss said this was going to be an assignment that was larger than usual. "No big deal," I replied, "I'm up to it."

AL: Up to it? Only up to my kneecaps, I should say. It's so hard to tell from up here, though.

K-ZOO NEWS: Huh? Who's there? The clouds are talking to me!

AL: Up here, son.

K-ZOO NEWS: Kabunga! You're an elephant, aren't you?

AL: I'm an African elephant, actually. To be a little more exact, my name is *Loxodonta africana,* but that's kind of hard even for an elephant to remember, so you can call me Al.

K-ZOO NEWS: Uh . . . uh . . .

AL: That's close. Put an *L* on the end, and you'll have my name.

K-ZOO NEWS: Uh . . . Al? Big, very big Al . . . ! I . . . uh . . . wonder if you'd . . . uh . . . mind questioning a few of my answers?

AL: Pardon?

K-ZOO NEWS: I mean answer a few of my questions. For an interview?

AL: Certainly.

K-ZOO NEWS: Let's start with the obvious. You're huge!

AL: You have profoundly stated the obvious. Well done! African elephants are the largest mammals that presently roam the face of the earth. An African elephant grows to be nineteen to twenty-five feet long and ten to thirteen feet high at the shoulders (that's higher than a basketball goal). Our tails grow to be as long as four feet, and we weigh 11,000 to 16,500 pounds (that's about the same as five or six compact cars).

K-ZOO NEWS: Sounds like you carry a lot of weight around here.

AL: True, very true. We can weigh as much as five times what a giraffe or rhinoceros does. Our ears are fan-shaped and can spread as far as five feet away from our heads. Both males and females grow tusks. Tusks grow continuously and can reach over eleven feet long. One-third of our tusks are imbedded in our upper jaw. Our skin can be over an inch and a half thick, but it is very sensitive.

K-ZOO NEWS: That's a lot of heft to heave!

AL: It is, and we carry it all around on our tiptoes!

K-ZOO NEWS: You what!?!!

AL: What looks like our knees are the bones that correspond to the human wrist. But our four feet combined cover an area of over three square feet, and the soles of our feet are specially designed to take our weight. Our soles expand beneath our weight as we walk to distribute the weight and take some of the burden from our leg bones.

K-ZOO NEWS: Well, bless my soul!

AL: Bless my sole! Our legs are composed of massive bones that lack marrow. Elephants' legs are extremely strong and are perfectly adapted for moving an elephant along at a good clip. An elephant can walk at about the same speed as a human (two to four miles per hour). If we're in a hurry, we can lope along at five to seven miles per hour for hours on end, and if we really get excited, we can run faster than the fastest human sprinter (almost nineteen miles per hour), but only for 300 feet or so. Elephants can't gallop or jump. This means walls are pretty much impassable for an elephant if it can't knock them down. But elephants are excellent climbers and can ascend slopes that are almost vertical.

K-ZOO NEWS: Where do you get that kind of energy?

AL: Duracell batteries.

K-ZOO NEWS: Huh?

AL: Just kidding. It's closer to solar and water power than electrical. You see, elephants are strict vegetarians, and we eat only leaves, twigs, and grass, which of course grow due to sun and water. We are also the only African animals besides the baboons that dig holes in the ground to get to water. We use our tusks to loosen dirt and use our trunks to dig holes deeper than you'd want to fall into. Digging holes helps elephants survive drought periods.

K-ZOO NEWS: Tell me about that trunk.

AL: Our trunks are extremely useful objects, and I highly recommend one. It can substitute for a hand for grasping things such as food but is also an excellent device for smelling and touching things. It comes in very handy for getting a drink. We suck nearly a bucketful of water fifteen inches up our trunks, close to the end of the trunk with the fingerlike projection at the tip, and then squirt the water into our mouths. Can I offer you a drink?

K-ZOO NEWS: Uh, no thanks. Not just now.

AL: OK. An elephant can pick a coin up from the floor with its trunk or lift a baby elephant over a fallen tree.

K-ZOO NEWS: Speaking of babies, do you have any children?

AL: Ah, yes! Li'l Al Junior was born just a few days ago—almost twenty-two months since his mother became pregnant. A lovely bundle of joy too! Weighed 220 pounds and was two-and-a-half feet tall.

K-ZOO NEWS: How old will he live to be?

AL: That really depends on his teeth.

K-ZOO NEWS: His teeth?

AL: Yes. Elephants go through five or six pairs of teeth in a lifetime. Each new set arrives at a different age. The last set of molars arrives at about the age of thirty-three years, and each tooth is the size of a small brick. After the age of sixty years or so, new teeth won't grow. Even a healthy elephant will die in the end from not being able to eat properly. The oldest known zoo elephant died at the age of sixty-five years. In the wild, an elephant usually dies earlier due to diseases, parasites, and humans.

K-ZOO NEWS: Humans?

AL: Yes. Elephants have no enemies in our natural habitat. But humans kill elephants for our ivory, and African elephants often are killed since of all elephants, we are the largest. But natural enemies don't exist. Even rhinoceroses recognize an African elephant as the superior animal. Very rarely will a rhino attack an elephant, and when it does, the rhino doesn't usually win.

K-ZOO NEWS: So, what do you do for fun?

AL: For fun. Well, we try to give subtle hints to the humans who move into our territory. A herd of elephants will often cover a newly laid road with twigs or pile twigs over low street signs. Sometimes we just pull a few telephone poles out of the ground.

K-ZOO NEWS: Well, Al, I appreciate the interview . . . It was big-hearted of you to spare the time. Until next time . . .

7—KZOO

Lighten Up!

K-ZOO NEWS: The boss said he had a really bright idea for an interview, and he sent me out here to find a firefly. So I'm in this field in the middle of the night holding my flashlight . . .

SPARKY: Uh, excuse me, mister. The fellows over there asked me to ask you if you could kill the flashlight 'cause it's kind of distracting the ladies, if ya' know what I mean.

K-ZOO NEWS: Oh, sorry. Didn't mean to put you in a bad light. Say, would you mind if I asked you a few questions for an interview?

SPARKY: You mean put me in the spotlight? Go ahead.

K-ZOO NEWS: I was wondering, are you really a fly?

SPARKY: No. Fireflies are beetles. We belong to a family that is made up of about 1,900 different species.

K-ZOO NEWS: Wow! There are 1,900 different types of fireflies?

SPARKY: Yup. Fireflies range in size from five millimeters to twenty-five millimeters (as big as an inch long). We have a flat, soft body that is dark brown or black, and usually we have orange or yellow markings.

K-ZOO NEWS: Well, let's get right to the heart of the matter. How do you do it?

SPARKY: Uh, do what?

K-ZOO NEWS: How do you light up like you do?

SPARKY: We carry around miniature Coleman© lanterns.

K-ZOO NEWS: Really? Wow!

SPARKY: Not too bright, are you? I was just kidding.

K-ZOO NEWS: Oh. Of course. I knew it all along.

SPARKY: Right. Our light source is under nervous control.

K-ZOO NEWS: Oh! So when you're nervous, you light up?

SPARKY: Uh . . . not exactly. Lighting up for us is the same as moving your left big toe. It's done through messages to the nervous system that cause special cells called photocytes to produce light. The light is generated by an organ made up of three layers. The deepest layer is made up of cells that contain microscopic crystals of uric-acid salt. The surfaces of the crystals reflect light outward.

K-ZOO NEWS: Wow! Kind of like a laser beam hitting a mirror, huh?

SPARKY: Uh, yeah, I guess. Whatever helps you to understand. The next layer out from the reflecting layer contains the photocytes. The photocytes are connected to a vast number of nerves. Each photocyte contains particles called mitochondria that supply the energy to activate the light-producing chemical luciferin.

K-ZOO NEWS: Awesome! Power enough to light up your whole body using your own personal nuclear reactor!

SPARKY: That's one way of looking at it—an odd way, but still a way of looking at it. The third layer is an outer layer of skin that is a transparent window.

K-ZOO NEWS: Can you produce X-rays and infrared rays?

SPARKY: No! We'd all die of cancer if we did that, wouldn't we?

K-ZOO NEWS: Shucks, not even ultraviolet rays?

SPARKY: Trying to get a tan, or what? Nothing like that. The light we produce is entirely safe, and all of our light is visible to the human eye. We aren't hiding anything, and we don't come with a surgeon general's warning.

K-ZOO NEWS: You must get pretty hot flipping your light on and off all the time. Ever have a meltdown?

SPARKY: Alas, another false idea started because of our name. Not only are fireflies not flies, but we don't come anywhere close to fire. Unlike your ordinary light bulb, which produces heat, the light from a firefly is completely cold; otherwise, you'd have fireflies bursting into flames in midair, or perhaps whole forests would be burned to the ground from miniature explosions at night.

Since no heat is produced, the light of the firefly is one of the most efficient forms of light production known to the world. Take your average light bulb, for instance. It is only about 3 percent efficient, since 97 percent of the energy released isn't light but heat! Most fireflies are 90 percent efficient, which means only 10 percent of the energy is wasted as something other than light.

K-ZOO NEWS: Wow! So you are the world's most efficient light bulb!

SPARKY: Yes, but there's a catch. It would take about 6,000 females of the most common type of firefly to produce a light as bright as the light from one candle.

K-ZOO NEWS: Oh. That's an awful lot of fireflies.

SPARKY: Well, on the brighter side, you have the firefly called *Pyrophorus noctilucus.* It only takes about forty of them to produce the same amount of light.

K-ZOO NEWS: But that's still a lot of fireflies. I always thought you were really bright.

SPARKY: That's probably because the light fireflies produce is along a wavelength that human eyes are most sensitive to. In fact, by the light of the brightest fireflies, a book can be easily read. The brightest fireflies are found in the tropical areas of India, Burma, Thailand, and Malaysia. One tropical type of firefly has eleven pairs of green lights and a red light in front. It has received the name of "railway worm."

K-ZOO NEWS: So what's the light all about, anyway?

SPARKY: One reason is to warn predators. Once a predator eats a firefly and finds out how bitter tasting we are, he'll remember not to ask for a light at his next meal. However, there are some frogs (with particularly poor taste) who gorge themselves on so many fireflies that they actually begin to glow themselves!

K-ZOO NEWS: I guess you could say that those fireflies had been de-lighted!

SPARKY: Not funny.

K-ZOO NEWS: My humblest apologies. Please continue.

SPARKY: The light also serves to turn on the ladies. Most types of fireflies produce flashes in certain patterns that distinguish one species from another.

K-ZOO NEWS: Cool! Kind of like a secret code, huh?

SPARKY: Uh, sure . . . When a female sees the males' signal, she turns on her lights in a pattern that lets the males know she's interested. The males usually have large, protruding eyes that help them see the light of the females. Usually the female's flashes are brighter than the male's. Timing, rate, duration, and intensity of flashes are all vital. For example, the North American firefly watches for a signal to appear exactly two seconds after his signal is given.

K-ZOO NEWS: Have to make some split-second decisions about dating, huh?

SPARKY: Uh, yeah . . . Anyway, when a male receives an answer, he heads off in the direction of the female. Once the male has found the partner, he touches her with his antennae to make sure she has the proper smell. And the rest, as they say, is history. Sometimes, when a full moon is out, fireflies reduce their signaling. We don't like the competition.

K-ZOO NEWS: So, tell me about the kids.

SPARKY: The larvae live on the ground and feast on slugs and snails by injecting a fluid that begins to digest the prey. Then the food is taken in through hollow mouthparts. Many adult fireflies don't eat. Those that do feed on pollen and nectar. But since most females can't fly, and most adult fireflies don't eat, the adult life of a firefly is a mere flash in the pan. However, the larval stage lasts several months or even years.

K-ZOO NEWS: Well, have you any other facts you'd like to enlighten us with?

SPARKY: Only one. In some tropical areas, certain types of fireflies gather at night in specific trees in large quantities. The amazing thing is not that they always gather in the same trees, but that all the fireflies flash in unison. For a fraction of a second, a jungle tree will burst into an eerie greenish glow against the black of the jungle sky and then disappear again.

K-ZOO NEWS: Ladies and gentlemen, there you have the amazing firefly.

Nature's Teddy Bear

K-ZOO NEWS: Hello, I'm your friendly news reporter interviewing the world's most popular animal. Would you say that was correct, sir?

COLBY: Well, yes, we koalas get a lot of attention. I guess we're what you could call "nature's teddy bear."

K-ZOO NEWS: May I quote you on that, sir?

COLBY: You certainly may.

K-ZOO NEWS: Thank you. There are some rumors going around that you are really just a toy come to life. How do you feel about such comments, and how do they affect you?

COLBY: You know, to tell you the truth, I don't mind being thought of as a toy come to life. I think the kids all love it!

K-ZOO NEWS: Tell me a little about your living quarters. Is it true you live in a high-rise?

COLBY: I suppose you could call it a high-rise. I actually tried getting my own home and settling down in a quiet neighborhood, but the neighbors didn't approve of my nocturnal (nighttime) habits. One lady in particular suspected me of spying on her, when all I was doing was eating some of the eucalyptus leaves from the tree in her backyard. She happened to have the best gum tree in the

whole neighborhood. Anyway, I had to move out, and now I simply curl up in the fork of a tree during the day.

K-ZOO NEWS: I understand your ancestors were almost wiped out. Would you like to comment on that?

COLBY: Well, there's not much to say, except that hunters were after their skins. I must admit we are rather defenseless and amiable creatures and have always been opposed to violence.

K-ZOO NEWS: Do you have any children?

COLBY: Yes, as a matter of fact, I do! My wife and I have one child every other year. The kids usually stay in Mom's pouch until they are six months old. Then the following six months are really rough for Mom, since Junior gets on Mom's back a lot. You often hear her saying, "Would you get off my back, Junior?"

K-ZOO NEWS: Is it true that your grandfather set a record for being the oldest koala?

COLBY: Yes, he did. He lived to a ripe old age, but most of our type live to be only twenty.

K-ZOO NEWS: I understand all koalas are very health conscious.

COLBY: Yes, we are. We never drink—not even water—and we definitely don't drink and drive! As a matter of fact, *koala* in the Aborigine language means "no drink." We don't smoke either, since forest fires are now the greatest threat to our lives!

K-ZOO NEWS: Many people say koalas have a distinct odor. How would you describe it?

COLBY: Well, as one famous koala put it, "We smell like a giant cough drop!"

K-ZOO NEWS: Thank you very much for your time, Mr. Cough Drop—uh, I mean, Mr. Koala, sir.

COLBY: You're welcome.

K-ZOO NEWS: This is your faithful reporter, reporting from the home of all koalas—Australia. Stay tuned. We'll be right back after these messages . . .

A Star Performance

K-ZOO NEWS: Hollywood, Hollywood! Yes, this is my chance! It's off to the stars for me. I just happened to be in the right place at the right time and overheard my boss muttering about an assignment on stars. Naturally I volunteered to take such a problem off his hands. Now I'm here at my interview location—a sandy beach with foamy ocean waves bubbling at my feet, beckoning me with five outstretched arms—What? Five arms! What's going on here?

STELLA: Are you referring to me?

K-ZOO NEWS: Who are you? I'm supposed to be having an interview here, so if you would buzz off, I'd be most grateful.

STELLA: What a coincidence! I was to have an interview here as well!

K-ZOO NEWS: Oh, no! Are you one of those . . . those . . . er . . . ur . . .

STELLA: Starfish! Yup, that's me.

K-ZOO NEWS: Something's fishy here!

STELLA: No, actually I'm not a fish at all. I belong to a group of wonderful creatures called echinoderms. The word *echinoderm* means "spiny-skinned." There are more than 2,000 different types of starfish, and probably many more are yet to be discovered!

K-ZOO NEWS: This interview is going to take longer than I had thought.

STELLA: Oh, no! Don't worry. Starfish are alike for the most part. I'll answer for all sea stars.

K-ZOO NEWS: Well, OK. But I won't be able to use my original interview questions. Let's see. Could you tell me why you have so many arms?

STELLA: So many? Dear me, I'm one of the less fortunate. I have only five arms, but some of my friends have as many as fifty. And if you think we have a lot of arms, you'd really be surprised at the number of feet we have.

K-ZOO NEWS: Please tell me. I love surprises.

STELLA: We have thousands of tube feet, which allow us to move surprisingly fast over sand. We move at a speed of two to six inches per minute!

K-ZOO NEWS: Humph, that's not so fast.

STELLA: Oh, yeah? Well, you try to coordinate thousands of feet. I've seen you humans get only two feet tangled up, and down you go. But have you ever seen a starfish trip? Have you?

K-ZOO NEWS: Well, no, I can't say that I have.

STELLA: Hey, it took me several years just to get to this interview!

K-ZOO NEWS: I'm sure! How do you coordinate your feet?

STELLA: Well, they work on a hydraulic system. That is, they are operated, or moved, by means of water. To get extra traction for climbing rocks or even climbing up the sides of aquarium windows, we lay down a sticky substance in front of us.

K-ZOO NEWS: What is it that you eat once you reach your food?

STELLA: Oh, just about anything we come across, alive or dead. We can pry open oysters by using constant pressure. Once the oyster's shell is a fraction of the way open (the width of a piece of cardboard will suffice), we can actually slip our stomach inside the oyster and eat it. I guess you'd call that eating out!

K-ZOO NEWS: Very funny! Please go on.

STELLA: As you can imagine, oyster farmers despise us. A young sea star will devour more than fifty oysters in a week. The farmers lose more than $200,000 annually because of starfish.

K-ZOO NEWS: That's incredible! How do starfish reproduce?

STELLA: There are several ways. We can multiply by dividing, for one. If one of our arms is cut off, we can grow a new arm back where the old arm was, and we will be just as good as new. Also, a new star will develop from each severed arm. The story is told of some foolish sailors who didn't like all the starfish they were catching in their fishing nets. So they took their knives and divided the stars into halves and threw them back into the ocean. What they didn't know was that each section grew into a new star, so they were simply multiplying their problems. Double trouble, you could say.

K-ZOO NEWS: Fascinating!

STELLA: Thank you. We can also multiply by laying eggs. We have been known to lay as many as two-and-a-half million eggs in a couple of hours.

K-ZOO NEWS: Wow! Why don't you tell me about how other starfish look. They don't all look like you, do they?

STELLA: Certainly not! Different species of stars vary greatly in looks. We can have anywhere from four to fifty arms, but most of us have five arms. Some starfish are very small and grow to be only a half-inch across, while others grow to be more than two feet across! Some have been as large as a car tire! Probably the most fascinating variation is the wide contrast of colors and markings. Starfish range in color from shades of brown to red, yellows, whites, purples, or greens. We also come in bright stripes, brilliant spots, or colorful patterns.

K-ZOO NEWS: If I wanted to find a starfish, where in the world would I look? The tropics?

STELLA: Incredibly, starfish are found in *all* the oceans of the world, but the largest number thrive in the North Pacific, not in the tropics. I tend to stay in fairly shallow water, but some types may be found at depths of more than 3,500 feet.

K-ZOO NEWS: One last question. I don't want to do you a bad turn, but what would happen to you if you were flipped onto your back?

STELLA: A common misconception is that a starfish would be helpless if placed on its back. Not true! We *can* right ourselves without any help.

K-ZOO NEWS: And with those flippant remarks, I'll sign off this interview.

Monster Guinea Pigs

K-ZOO NEWS: Well, friends, today I'll be interviewing a rodent found only in South America. It'll probably be some furry little mouse or something. Doesn't sound too exciting, if you ask me. What I want in a job is excitement, and I'm afraid mice just don't send chills up my spine. Now take, for example, that monster guinea pig over . . . there. He looks . . . uh . . . very excited . . . and very hungry!

CHAPPY: Excuse me, señor. I could not help but overhear, and I feel I must correct you. Your misinformation may cause thousands to believe false facts! I am *not* a monster guinea pig. I am a capybara.

K-ZOO NEWS: Uh . . . er . . . really?

CHAPPY: Sí. And you need not be afraid. We capybaras are vegetarians and really quite harmless to people in general.

K-ZOO NEWS: But you look like a guinea pig I once saw in a cage at a pet store—only a few sizes larger. You're huge!

CHAPPY: Ah, sí, I will admit that I am huge. But capybaras have an image to keep up. You see, being the largest rodent on earth requires us to grow a bit bigger than other rodents.

K-ZOO NEWS: How much is a bit bigger?

CHAPPY: We are about eight times longer than your average guinea pig, and 200 or more times heavier. We grow to be four feet long and two feet high at the shoulder and weigh up to 130 pounds.

K-ZOO NEWS: That's a *bit* bigger? If a man were to grow eight times larger and 200 times heavier than average, he'd be about forty-six feet tall and weigh about 36,000 pounds. That's a *lot* bigger! And all you eat is grass?

CHAPPY: No. Not just grass, although our name means "master of the grasses." We feed on grass, water plants, and woody plants. We gnaw on the trunks of some trees just like a beaver does. Sometimes we don't like eating alone, so we'll join a herd of domestic cattle and graze in their company. We'll even raid watermelon crops, cornfields, and rice and sugar-cane plantations. The farmers get a little hostile, though, when we start eating up their profits.

K-ZOO NEWS: How hostile?

CHAPPY: They kill us.

K-ZOO NEWS: That *is* hostile.

CHAPPY: Sí. They are very protective of those leafy green things that grow on their property, and when they see us doing a taste test, they get pretty violent.

K-ZOO NEWS: So what do you do?

CHAPPY: What would *you* do? We run away, of course. When we're threatened, we run off and leap into water.

K-ZOO NEWS: Why water?

CHAPPY: Because capybaras are perfectly fit for water life. We swim and dive easily and can stay underwater for several minutes. We have short webs between our toes, and these help us swim. When we are disturbed, we usually head for the river, where will jump in and swim away from the enemy. By swimming completely submerged for several minutes, we get a more comfortable distance between ourselves and the fellow looking for a good meal.

K-ZOO NEWS: You mean the farmer eats what ate his crops?

CHAPPY: Sí, at least sometimes. In fact, men are our worst enemies. Jaguars and crocodiles consider us good food, but men kill many capybaras. I guess we have good taste, because humans like to eat us. To keep from being killed, we have had to change the way we live. Where capybaras have not been hunted or harassed by people, we travel and eat during the day, but we have turned almost nocturnal (we come out only at night) in the areas where we have been hunted. In those areas we come out at dawn and dusk to browse, but by day we keep to our hideouts.

K-ZOO NEWS: Your hideouts? You mean like secret underground passages and tunnels?

CHAPPY: No, nothing that elaborate. Some capybaras have hideouts that are deep burrows in a steep riverbank. Others simply use hollows made deep within thickets that are impenetrable by people.

K-ZOO NEWS: How about children?

CHAPPY: Children can't get into the thickets either.

K-ZOO NEWS: No, that's not what I meant.

CHAPPY: Oh. Well, I like children. They are very nice to have around.

K-ZOO NEWS: What I meant was, do you have any?

CHAPPY: Oh, sí! Eight of them.

K-ZOO NEWS: Eight!

CHAPPY: Sí. Every year a capybara mother will have two to eight children. Our children usually do not need much attention. After a very short time they can eat without their mother bringing all their food to them. But a capy family is a happy family—heh, heh—and usually the younger children stay at home, where they eat together and sleep together as a family. They will grow up to have the typical good looks that all capybaras possess—short muzzle, very small eyes and ears, and a hairy coat ranging from brown to reddish yellow. We have four toes on our front feet and three on the back.

K-ZOO NEWS: Well, gracias, mister "master of the grasses," for the interview.

CHAPPY: Now I must get home. I promised the señora that we would go out to eat tonight.

K-ZOO NEWS: I hope you enjoy your dinner. Until next time . . .

Doxiongmao

K-ZOO NEWS: Hi! I am standing here in what looks like an ominous and dense bamboo forest in the far reaches of western China. I believe there is an animal around here that I'm supposed to interview. Let's see. My assignment sheet says his name is *doxiongmao.* And that's just his *first* name! Do you know what that is? Man, I've never heard of such a thing. Oops! What's this I'm tripping over? Hmmm, looks like a panda. Excuse me, sir. Sir!

DOXIE: Rrrr . . . Huh? What's this? *Yawnnnn.* Who are you, anyway?

K-ZOO NEWS: I'm an interviewer, and I was wondering if you had seen a *doxiongmao* around here recently?

DOXIE: Yes, sir. You've found yourself one!

K-ZOO NEWS: You? Why, you're just a panda!

DOXIE: I'm *just* a panda. Would you care to rephrase that?

K-ZOO NEWS: Well, er—

DOXIE: *Doxiongmao* is my Chinese name. It means "large bear-cat."

K-ZOO NEWS: Oh. In that case, would you mind being interviewed?

DOXIE: Mind? An interview? Do you realize what time of day it is, sonny? Why, it's—uh—

K-ZOO NEWS: It's the middle of the afternoon, sir!

DOXIE: Oh. In that case, maybe I should get up. But an interview? Well, OK. But hurry it up, or I'll miss my nap.

K-ZOO NEWS: Oh, yes, of course. Say, I don't believe I've ever seen a panda in my backyard. Could you explain that?

DOXIE: Yes, I think I could explain that. Either you don't have a very nice backyard, or you don't live in the deep bamboo forests of western China. All pandas live there because there's plenty of bamboo to eat. Eat! Yes, I am hungry. You wouldn't happen to have any bamboo on you, would you?

K-ZOO NEWS: Uh, no, 'fraid not. I'm trying to quit.

DOXIE: Ha, ha! Very funny! Bamboo is really quite good for you. At least if you're a panda. We eat the whole thing—stalk, leaves, and shoots.

K-ZOO NEWS: Is that all you eat? Just bamboo?

DOXIE: Oh, dear me, no! Only bamboo? What a ridiculous notion. Pandas will eat fish, rodents, and other types of small animals, if we get the chance. Even interviewers, if they wake us up in the middle of the day.

K-ZOO NEWS: Huh?

DOXIE: Just kidding!

K-ZOO NEWS: Whew! Say, what do you drink? I understand the ground is snow-covered much of the time here. Do you get your water from the snow?

DOXIE: Snow? Interesting concept. No, we don't. If we ate snow, we'd use up a large amount of valuable energy by using our body heat to melt the snow in our stomachs. No, sir. We get most of our water from the bamboo. You see, bamboo is about 50 percent water. And since 99 percent of our diet consists of the bamboo stem, branches, and leaves, we get an adequate amount of water from them. Even so, we do take a drink once or twice a day.

K-ZOO NEWS: You seem to be concerned with saving energy. Would you comment on that?

DOXIE: Yes. Energy is extremely valuable, and pandas try to waste as little as possible. For example, we try to limit the number of calorie-expensive activities. We prefer to travel over moderate terrain rather than up and down steep slopes. Also, when we're startled or frightened, we trot off rapidly instead of tearing off in a frenzied gallop.

K-ZOO NEWS: Interesting! Um, could you tell me if the way you walk has anything to do with energy conservation?

DOXIE: The way we walk?

K-ZOO NEWS: Yes. You walk with remarkable ease and silence and with a sort of rolling, diagonal gait.

DOXIE: No, I don't think that has anything to do with energy conservation. Now please, don't poke fun at me! You don't look so graceful when you're walking either! Shall I tell the audience which one of us was tripping over his microphone cord and blindly walking over sleeping pandas earlier?

K-ZOO NEWS: That's OK. Why don't we switch to another subject. Do you have a family?

DOXIE: Oh, yes! I have a beautiful wife and two children. Our first kids! They are so precious! Weighed only five ounces apiece when they were born.

K-ZOO NEWS: Wow! Only five ounces? They must eat a lot to get to be your size!

DOXIE: Are you saying I'm fat?

K-ZOO NEWS: Well, er . . . you do sleep all day.

DOXIE: Yes, I do. But if you had been considerate enough to ask, you would have known that pandas stay up for ten to twelve hours a night eating. Yes, ten to twelve hours! Don't look so shocked, buddy! You'd have to stay up that long too if you had to eat thirty pounds of food in order to maintain a weight of 300 pounds.

K-ZOO NEWS: Yes, I'm sure I would. Would you be so kind as to describe yourself to our reading audience?

DOXIE: Well, certainly I look a bit like a bear, except I have a white chubby body. I have a black shoulder band, black legs, and matching black eyepatches. My tail is very short, and my head is large and round with a white face and small black ears sprouting from the top.

K-ZOO NEWS: Who are your closest relatives?

DOXIE: Well, there's Sally and Ja . . .

K-ZOO NEWS: No, no. I mean what animal?

DOXIE: Oh. Zoologists are playing ping-pong with that idea. They can't decide whether I'm more of a bear or more of a raccoon, or if I'm something totally different. So I can't really tell you who my closest relatives are, since that would give away our secret. To put it in the scientists' words: "The systematic affinity of the panda is under altercation and litigation at this point in our deciphering of the amassed evidence, but on the feeble basis of anatomical, biochemical, and paleontological evidence, the taxonomic position remains equivocal." No wonder they can't figure out what I am! Nobody can understand what they are talking about! Equivocal? The best they can do is say I'm *equivocal,* huh? Boy, I don't get any respect!

K-ZOO NEWS: I see that! Well, not knowing what you are could certainly be perplexing and possibly lead to a personality disorder.

DOXIE: I suppose it could! And it might be permanent.

K-ZOO NEWS: Say, I understand you're a pretty popular animal—one of the favorites with the kids.

DOXIE: Well, I guess you could say that. One zookeeper in New York said that for every person who asks him about an aardvark, 30,000 people ask him where they can find the panda. Pandas are also mentioned in ancient Chinese books that are more than 2,000 years old. In fact, in times past, we were considered a prize possession. A panda's skull was found in a royal tomb dated back to 179 B.C.

K-ZOO NEWS: I very much appreciate this interview, and I do hope you don't miss your nap on my account. Now, where is that Jeep? I just parked it behind a large cluster of bamboo, and now it seems to have disappeared . . .

Prickly Football

K-ZOO NEWS: That's right, folks, a pig! I'm off to interview a hog. A mud-wallower and scum-swallower is what I'm in for today. There can't be any doubt about it, because the boss sent me out here into the country areas. All I have to do is wait for the pig to show itself.

HODGES: Uh, pardon me, sir. I hate to interrupt your intensely fascinating speech, but I am to be interviewed in the very spot that you are occupying.

K-ZOO NEWS: No, you must be mistaken. I'm to interview a hog here, so if you'd kindly move along—

HODGES: A hog? Are you an interviewer?

K-ZOO NEWS: Yes. Are you a hog?

HODGES: Quite right, sir.

K-ZOO NEWS: Why, you're just a prickly football. I can't interview a football when I'm supposed to interview a pig!

HODGES: I've never been so insulted in all my life! I am a hedgehog and quite obviously not a football.

K-ZOO NEWS: A hedgehog? Really? You look like a porcupine.

HODGES: Well, yes, that's entirely possible. You see, where other mammals have fur, I have spines. The spines cover my back and make a sharp outfit, if I do say so. Between the spines I have a few coarse hairs, and my head and belly are covered with hair, the same as other mammals.

K-ZOO NEWS: So what is the point of all those prickles?

HODGES: Well, let me be blunt. These spines become immensely useful for keeping enemies away.

K-ZOO NEWS: Really?

HODGES: Oh, yes. Our highly developed skin muscles can hold the quills quite erect when we are being attacked. Then we simply roll into a perfect ball with all our vital parts inside and nothing but thousands of prickles poking out in every direction.

K-ZOO NEWS: Good idea!

HODGES: Trying to attack a rolled-up hedgehog would be like diving into a swimming pool filled with sharpened pencils—not very comfortable. Occasionally we come across a really dumb carnivore who's just dying to have a hedgehog for lunch. If the carnivore does kill the hedgehog, it will find some of the quills in its flesh, because our quills break off easily. Although the beast has gotten a meal, it may be one of its last. As the animal uses its muscles, the spines work their way in deeper and deeper. One day, perhaps many days after the death of the hedgehog, a spine may reach a vital organ and kill the previous victor. Hedgehogs aren't gracious losers.

K-ZOO NEWS: Say . . . uh . . . just out of curiosity . . . um . . . how long are your spikes?

HODGES: Oh, about an inch long.

K-ZOO NEWS: Oh.

HODGES: But our spines are useful for more than simple protection. They cushion us from falls and are quite useful in courtship.

K-ZOO NEWS: You mean you use your spikes when you're on

a date with a lady hedgehog?

HODGES: Oh, sure! During courtship the males start a dance by whirling around and around the female with all our quills rattling loudly. At first the female plays hard to get and refuses to dance, but suddenly she'll get caught up in the fun and start whirling and rattling too!

K-ZOO NEWS: So does this ever lead to marriage?

HODGES: But of course! Hedgehogs have between two and eight children at a time. The kids are born with rubbery spines, but after about twenty days the spines harden and become fierce weapons. When they grow up, they look just like me—small, round ears; squat, pudgy body that's ten to twelve inches long and five to six inches high. They'll have excellent hearing and sharp smell, but only average sight.

K-ZOO NEWS: What do you eat?

HODGES: Oh, all sorts of insects, slugs, snails, small rodents, birds, frogs, snakes—

K-ZOO NEWS: Snakes?

HODGES: Sure. What's wrong with snakes? Their bark is worse than their bite.

K-ZOO NEWS: Snakes don't bark.

HODGES: Precisely! And their bite is harmless. We have no qualms about snake hunting. A snake finds it nearly impossible to defend itself against a hedgehog. Think about it! It can't coil around us to squeeze us to death. The snake would impale itself on our spines. And not only would it be hard for a snake to bite us, but we wouldn't care if it did. Hedgehogs are immune to snake venom.

K-ZOO NEWS: Imagine that!

HODGES: I don't have to imagine it; it's true.

K-ZOO NEWS: Oh, yes, of course. Where do you live?

HODGES: Well, hedgehogs can live just about anywhere. We flourish in the deserts of Algeria and Afghanistan. We live it up in the high-rises of the Alps and Caucasus mountains. And we survive the frigid cold of Siberia. In the cold regions, we hibernate during the winter, but we are active all year round in the milder climates. Gardeners like us because we feed on insects that would damage their crops. So there are many hedgehogs in rural areas. We are inoffensive creatures and come out mostly at dusk, so we don't bother farmers much.

K-ZOO NEWS: Well, thank you for the interview. I've never interviewed a football with spikes before.

HODGES: I thought you weren't going to insult me again.

K-ZOO NEWS: I never said that!

HODGES: Now see here . . .

Solar Snowball

K-ZOO NEWS: Hello, all you lucky, warm readers at home! I've made some cold comments in my life, but all my comments will be cold today. I'm standing in the frozen northern region of our earth, and, to be quite honest, I don't like it very much!

POLLY: Excuse me, mister!

K-ZOO NEWS: Huh? Who's there?

POLLY: Would you mind telling me what you're doing on *my* ice floe? Besides shivering, that is.

K-ZOO NEWS: Uh, well, I think I was just leaving . . .

POLLY: Really?

K-ZOO NEWS: Actually, I was looking for a polar bear to interview, but I might change my mind.

POLLY: Well, it looks like you've found one.

K-ZOO NEWS: May I ask where you live?

POLLY: Sure, go right ahead. Whatever makes you happy. I'll just sit here and listen.

K-ZOO NEWS: Huh?

POLLY: I'll listen while you ask me where I live.

K-ZOO NEWS: Oh. Where *do* you live?

POLLY: Here.

K-ZOO NEWS: Here? Could you be a little more specific?

POLLY: We polar bears just wander around up here in the northern limits of the globe. You can normally find us on drifting oceanic ice. As a matter of fact, a brave friend of mine was found drifting on an ice floe way out by Newfoundland. We simply go where the food is. I guess you could say we follow our diet!

K-ZOO NEWS: Hmmm. A sense of humor too! And what might your diet be?

POLLY: The ringed seal is our favorite food. Curious little critters. They make breathing holes in the ice. We scoop the snow out of the holes so we can get to them. Mind you, we backfill the hole a little so it doesn't look like it's been bothered. Then we sit and wait for our order to arrive.

K-ZOO NEWS: Wait? How long?

POLLY: Quite a long time, actually. Polar bears are known for their patience. We sit there until a seal sticks its head above water, and then we grab it. That's all there is to it! But it does take patience. If we aren't in the mood for baby-sitting holes in the ice, we'll eat fish, kelp, grass, and caribou.

K-ZOO NEWS: Caribou, huh? They run, don't they?

POLLY: You *are* a genius. Yes, of course they run.

K-ZOO NEWS: So how do you catch them?

POLLY: Our whitish fur serves as excellent camouflage against ice and snow. We just sneak up on them, and when we're close enough, we charge them. We can run up to twenty-five miles per hour over snow and ice for short distances and can run ten miles per hour for a long time.

K-ZOO NEWS: How do you manage a steady speed of ten miles per hour? I can't take even two steps on this ice without pounding the ground with my backside!

POLLY: Polar bears are specially equipped with broad, furry feet, which you probably lack. The fur makes us very surefooted. It clings to any tiny break in the ice. Furry feet also help keep our toes from freezing.

K-ZOO NEWS: I can't believe that a gigantic, fur-covered snowball like you can zoom around on this ice with no problem.

POLLY: Gigantic, fur-covered snowball, huh? I've been called a white bear, a water bear, a sea bear, and an ice bear. But never a fur-covered snowball!

K-ZOO NEWS: Well, pardon my words, but you are huge!

POLLY: You think I'm big? You should have seen my great-great-grandfather! He weighed 1,700 pounds and was eleven feet tall when he stood on his hind legs! An average adult male bear will weigh about 900 pounds and a female about 700 pounds—although it's not uncommon to find a polar bear that weighs over half a ton (1,000 pounds). We're about five feet high at the shoulders when we're on all fours, but an average polar bear can stand to a height of eight feet. Say, how much do you weigh? Looks like you could use a few ringed seals!

K-ZOO NEWS: Uh, no thanks. I think I'll pass. Do you swim at all?

POLLY: Only if we have to. We are big, but we do have enemies, and we aren't fast swimmers. Three miles an hour is our average speed in the water. I'm ashamed to say it, but in the water, even the ringed seals will sometimes gang up on us! Even so, one polar bear was seen swimming like mad 200 miles from land! Perhaps his ice floe had melted.

K-ZOO NEWS: Tell me more!

POLLY: OK! How about the bear facts?

- One swipe of our paw can be fatal to almost any animal.
- We can leap over six-foot-high fences in a single bound.
- We're one of the largest of all land carnivores (meat-eaters). We're also the only land mammal that ventures this far north.
- We can smell food or enemies at a distance of up to ten miles away! (It may take us an hour to get to the food, but we know it's there.)
- Polar bears aren't really white. The truth is, our fur is transparent. The whitish color is simply an illusion produced by the rough surface inside each hollow hair. Our skin is actually black! Because of this, we soak up the sunlight like a big solar sponge. Our dark skin greedily captures the warm sun rays directed there by our hollow hairs.

K-ZOO NEWS: Well, my solar snowball, I must be going. And thank you for the interview! So long until next time . . .